CU01508959

Network better

Jeremy Marchant

Practical Inspiration
PUBLISHING

First published in Great Britain by Practical Inspiration
Publishing, 2018

ISBN 978-1-78860-051-4

Practical Inspiration
PUBLISHING

Contents

IV What comes next?

I   Fundamentals

1 Introduction

1 In the beginning

Story: Maggie (1)

Maggie was one of two directors of a small business. The directors knew that business networking was an important part of their strategy for growing the business, but only Andy actually did any.

As a business, they needed more clients, and they needed their services to be more widely known in the local community. They both recognised that Maggie should network with other businesses.

It quickly became apparent that Maggie was highly resistant to the idea. She agreed she should do it. Deep down, she wanted to do it. But the idea of walking into a room full of people she didn't know filled her with little short of terror.

Maggie is the inspiration for this book. As Maggie and I talked about what her reservations were, and how realistic they were, she was identifying the problems that many people have when it comes to business networking.

We had quite a long chat, during which we uncovered that her real reservations were not those on the surface.

As I'll show later, when we want to change our behaviour in any part of our lives, we need to change the beliefs and feelings *we have about that behaviour. If we don't change those beliefs and feelings, it's not really surprising that the old behaviour persists.*

We create our feelings and beliefs about the world from our experiences of it. The best way of changing our beliefs and feelings, therefore, is to have new experiences. So, I suggested to Maggie that she go to a particular event in a week or so's time. I knew this event would be laid back to the point of being horizontal. It would be the least stressful business networking event one could possibly imagine.

Because she is an honourable woman, I knew that if she said she would go, she would. So I made sure I didn't leave her office until she had undertaken to grasp the nettle.

Later, I had a word with the organiser of the event. I asked him to do as much as he could to make Maggie's experience as stress-free as possible. He promised to look out for her and to introduce her to some people.

I also discovered that a business colleague intended to go to the event and asked her to look after Maggie too. I knew my colleague would make an effort to ensure Maggie met some people and she'd support Maggie.

I was unable to go to the event myself. Later, I had some feedback from my co-conspirators who reported that Maggie had attended and had been very nervous. But she stayed the course. And, naturally, as soon as she had done it once, she knew she could do it again.

We shall catch up with Maggie in the last topic of this book.

There will be some people reading this who need do no more than put the book down, sally forth with Maggie in mind, remembering the advice the witches gave Macbeth—

> *Be bloody, bold, and resolute…*
> *Be lion-mettled, proud.*

—and get on with it. For those needing a little more detail, the rest of this book beckons.

2 Your objectives in networking

This book starts with Maggie, her fears and experiences, and how, at the end of the day, she became a demon networker.

But really it is about you, with your experiences. It's about how you can get more of whatever it is you want to get from networking—without necessarily spending any more time or money. It is about doing it differently and doing it better.

I must stress that, although I home in on the 'networking event' as the forum in which you talk about your business, its products and services, and yourself, everything in the book is relevant in whatever context you are talking to others.

It is remarkably difficult to get what you want if you don't know what you want. And, even harder when you realise that what you should be aiming for is not what you want. It's what your business *needs*—which may not be what you personally want. The obvious example is that what your business needs you to do is to network well with other business people—something you may be reluctant to do.

To start with, I suggest it is really worth thinking about your objectives. Although what you *want* is interesting to you, it is a snare and a delusion. The important questions are: What do you *need*? and what does your business *need* (you to do)?

For most business people, the primary objective of networking is to get more clients. But it could be many other things, such as research, looking for a business partner, or just socialising (running a one-person band can be lonely). It may even be to look for a supplier!

This book is for you if you are a business person at a networking event needing more clients. It's equally for you if:

○ you are networking internally in a large organisation

○ you work in the public sector, where networking is a dark art from which riffraff like me are usually excluded

○ you are in the third sector where networking is often about finding donors, both of money and time.

There is nothing that is specific only to small and medium-sized businesses (SMEs), or the public sector, or charities or anyone else. It all applies to everyone at work.

Ultimately, my objective is to convince you that networking is all about the quality of the *relationships* we have with other people.

3 Does the world really need another book on business networking?

There is a plethora of books on the subject, yet I believe this book addresses two areas that are not usually covered well, or at all, in books on business networking.

Firstly, it considers how to use our emotional intelligence (EI) best when networking. Most books on networking are strictly behavioural. 'Do this', 'do that'. This is necessary, for sure, but it isn't sufficient. After all, business networking is about relating to people. It is *only* about relating to people, in fact. For most business people, it is the only activity that solely relies on their capacity to form and nurture relationships with other people in order to be successful.

In networking, if we are to develop good working relationships with others, we have to trade more than cold data about ourselves and our businesses with each other. For people who have any reservations at all about forming relationships—particularly business relationships—it can be daunting to realise that they are going to have to go into their emotions if their businesses are to thrive. And it isn't enough to delegate this to a colleague, though that is better than nothing.

I am sure the anxiety generated by *anticipating* doing it is far worse than the anxiety of *actually* doing it. And the anxiety around doing it fades away quickly on repetition and practice, as Maggie found.

In any case, it is not a binary on/off situation. It is not that one is either completely inept at developing business relationships or otherwise a complete star—someone who attracts titans of industry like a flame attracts moths. We are all somewhere on a continuum between those two extremes. We slip and slide around our position on the continuum according to how we feel on any day and depending on who we have to work with. But all of us can do it better. We learn subconsciously and, in a fundamental area like relationships with other human beings, almost whether we want to or not. Getting a little bit better is easy, so it is only necessary to carry on getting a little better.

It is all about understanding oneself and one's colleagues, both intellectually, for want of a better word, and emotionally. And then using that understanding to help others and to help them to help us. So, relationship building (which is what we need EI for) and networking in general are important parts of doing business rather than just annoying distractions.

Secondly, this book addresses the question,

OK, I'm doing everything the book tells me, so how come it isn't working?

Most people, other than the true novices, don't really need more instructions. People may need some *different* things to do, but what most people need is help to sort out why what they are currently doing isn't working.

The book therefore describes what to do—explicitly but concisely stating best practice, providing approaches, techniques and tools that people can use to network more effectively. It gives chapter and verse on why I recommend these approaches, techniques and tools and not others. There are some good books—for example, *The World's Best Known Marketing Secret* (by Ivan Misner and others)—which go into a lot more practical detail about what to do.

But the main thrust of this book relates to the reasons why networkers struggle at networking events. It turns out there is a surprisingly large number of reasons, and each networker has their own specific set of issues they should work on.

Incidentally, I am not going to apologise for using words like 'issue' and 'problem'. We are all told we must communicate about our businesses positively. But, in truth, if someone is doing something that isn't working, and they want to do it better, they have a problem. Then, doing something different may also be a problem, at least until it starts working. Tarting it up by referring to 'opportunities' and 'challenges' is not helpful. In all aspects of our lives, we would be happier if we more often called a spade a spade.

The book does not address internet networking. The subject deserves a book of its own. However, most people use internet facilities to network to some extent and there is much in this book that can be transported across, though I would caution doing so unthinkingly. The absence of face-to-face communication and the absence, usually, of dialogue in real time do demand a modified or different approach.

4 How to use this book

I don't expect you to believe anything in this book…

…but if you're prepared to give the ideas house-room—thinking about how they could help you, and thinking about how they already help others—I am sure you will find the book useful.

o Part 1 covers the fundamentals of emotionally intelligent networking.

o Part 2 suggests, very politely, that what you thought you were doing well, you could do better.

o Part 3 addresses the many ways in which people find their networking isn't working. It suggests things you are doing—or thinking or feeling—that you really should consider replacing with different actions, or thoughts or feelings.

o Part 4 points the way forward with purposeful one-to-one meetings. Parts 1–3 are all relevant and applicable here, too.

Some 139 short chapters, called topics, make up these parts, and are referred to in bold, for example, **5**.

Section 8 explains the importance of stories for every successful networker and this book contains over forty. Many of the stories are true, but I have anonymised the participants, changing their names, professions and in some cases gender. There's a story index at the back of the book.

Tweaking behaviours is only going to go so far in raising your game. More important is your attitude, or your approach, if you prefer. Attitude is the mix of thoughts and beliefs, and of emotions and feelings that operate all together, influencing each other in complex feedback loops, thereby generating behaviour (see **35**).

Sometimes, one's attitude is not all it could be. Usually, people have never really thought about what attitude they should have in the first place: what attitude would be the most useful one to have. In fact, one's attitude, one's approach, can have a profound effect on anything one does that requires at least one other person, whether it is networking, working with a partner to defuse an argument, setting up a joint venture or anything else.

The general instruction is: the actions you need to address first are those you think are least applicable to you. And, certainly, those you would rather not do are the ones you have to do.

The book faces up to the reasons why people like Maggie are resistant to some or all of this, and focusses on helping them deal with their resistance. Although a book in itself cannot overcome someone's resistance, the author can do his damnedest to help them do the overcoming. When you know what is going on for you and for other business people—and why—you are simply empowered to be a better business person in *every* domain of activity, including networking.

In short, the book aims to give readers an understanding of, and insight into, how and why emotional intelligence is essential for optimum networking.

Finally, I hope this book encourages, amuses and entertains.

2 What is networking, really?

5 Networking—why bother?

'All businesses need customers.'

'Business are just people.' (Actually, we shall see in **36** this isn't really true.)

'People buy from people.'

'We trust those we know and like.'

These and other commonplaces swirl around the world of marketing. Most people pay lip service to them, but few really put them into action, preferring instead to rely on processes that are familiar but for which there is little evidence, and on beliefs that are often counterproductive.

What does it mean to say, 'People buy from people'? Surely people buy the products and services that are sold to them. A robot could do as well. What are the consequences for you, if you believe that; or if you don't?

How about 'We trust those we know and like'? How do I know if anyone trusts me? How much harder would it be to develop business relationships with people if you think they might not trust you? Would you go about it differently?

'All businesses need customers.' We know that businesses can acquire customers in a variety of ways: advertising, cold calling, direct marketing and the rest. Arguably, the best way to get a customer is when a third party (preferably one of your existing customers) refers someone who trusts them to you. The next best way is when someone who isn't a customer—but does know you, understands what you do and likes and trusts you—refers someone who trusts them to you.

Even though this is what everyone wants to have happen, it happens spontaneously only extremely rarely. It needs to be encouraged and facilitated. This is what this book is about. Before you get to that idyllic stage of sitting back, fielding all the phone calls from people who have been recommended to contact you, there are several prior stages to go through:

a   going to 'networking events' or finding something else to do that gives you useful contacts

b   networking with those contacts

c   developing working relationships with some of these, and going on to develop referral relationships with a few of those

d   nurturing and maintaining those relationships—in other words, giving to those relationships.

Many business people are reluctant to go for the 'people angle' in business. The 'people angle' is essentially the one about working with people to get customers and clients (who are also people, of course). I suspect most people are reluctant because they are scared that, if they do find out how to do it, it will be too hard and they will fail. So they retreat into their comfort zone. Actually, it's only risky (to the extent that it is risky at all) if it is not done well enough, but that is true of everything in life.

At this point, I must stress that networking is only a means to an end. It isn't the end itself. The ends are the productive business relationships that can be developed as a result of networking. And the point of those relationships is that they deliver the best leads and the best referrals to possible clients. Or they help in your research, or they find you a supplier, or whatever.

Here, I shall just point out that, if your contact John talks about you to his colleague Jane on the basis that he thinks you can help her because he understands what you do, and suggests to her she contact you, that is a 'referral'. Anything less is a 'lead'.

There is an interesting question here, namely: in whose interest is John doing this? Jane's or yours? Or his?

Advocacy is a step up from that and happens when John discusses with Jane what her needs are and then explains to her why you are a good fit.

Networking is really just talking to a lot of people with the purpose of building business relationships with a small number of them. Sarah Owen was a master franchisee of the Referral Institute UK (now Asentiv UK) and a co-author of the bestselling book *The World's Best Known Marketing Secret*. She says, 'You have to kiss a lot of frogs'. There isn't the time to build business relationships with everyone we meet and, further, many of the people whom we meet are not in a position to help us, nor can we help them.

Imagine walking into a room of, say, thirty men (and I mean men), all with their backs turned to you as you walk in, each engaged in apparently fervent conversation with other people, all of whom have apparently known them intimately for decades. They're probably laughing heartily at each other's jokes. Many people who don't network view the idea as the stuff of nightmares. But, as Maggie showed, once you have done it, you will find it increasingly easy to do it again and to do it better.

Getting over that initial anxiety is all about state management— managing one's emotional state in order to perform optimally, even if optimally on the first few occasions isn't the best you are capable of. Although there are physical exercises you can do to lower tension and so on, in practice state management is about your beliefs and emotions. To get over these requires emotional intelligence, not instructions.

The answer to the question 'Networking—why bother?' is that, even allowing for travel time and the time spent eating an indifferent meal (if offered), networking events provide the quickest way to get the most raw material. But, of course, do not neglect your contact books (both business and personal) and any other techniques you have to generate candidates for relationship building. The aim is to get a good set of people with whom to do the 'after the event' stuff that I kick off in section 16.

A small network of business relationships, in which all parties are committed to referral as a way of delivering good leads to each other, should be an essential component of any business's attempts to get customers. And networking is the activity that generates those parties.

For some businesses, referral need be the only component of their marketing strategy. The extent to which this process plays a part in any particular business is a function of:

○   the nature of the services and goods their business provides

○   the nature of the people who will buy those goods and services

○   the market into which the business is selling

○   the business's position in the business cycle (startup, growth, mature growth)—the earlier in the cycle, the more networking you need to do.

Easing up the networking too much when you think you have enough clients is tempting but a bad move. Where is the next lot of clients going to come from? It's true that some of them will come from the relationships you have set up by then. But they only deliver a certain amount of work. For the rest you need to do more networking and more relationship building and, in particular, the maintenance and nurturing of your existing relationships.

It may not be as bad as the Red Queen advised Alice in *Through the Looking-Glass*—

> '…it takes all the running you can do, to keep in the same place. If you want to get somewhere else, you must run at least twice as fast as that!'

—but resting on your laurels is fatal.

It is worth thinking at the outset what the purpose of your business could be. I cover this in more detail later but, for now, here's a provocative suggestion:

The purpose of your business should be to get clients.

You could argue that the purpose of your business is to deliver a good professional service to your clients. But, what if prospects were *entitled to expect* you to be able to do that, and the real purpose was something else? Shouldn't your clients be entitled to expect you to be a competent professional? Shouldn't I be entitled to expect my accountant to be able to do my books and communicate with HMRC as well as I need (which he does)? And shouldn't my graphic designer be able to deliver compelling, yet stylish designs as befits my business (he does)?

Suppose a purpose is something that, if you did it well, it enabled your business to deliver a good professional service. The services become *outcomes* of your business. Not the purpose. More clients is the single most important thing a business needs if it is to survive, so why not make getting them the purpose of your business? Delivering the service to a particular client is then an *outcome*, a consequence of achieving the purpose of getting them on board.

I raise this here because a distressingly large number of business people seem to think that networking is something they do when they haven't anything better to do. Apart from their non-attendance letting down all the other people at the event, this attitude minimises the chance of getting anything at all from networking. Networking is clearly not going to take the bulk of any business person's time, but I believe that networking and the consequent development of referral relationships is the single most important thing a business person should be doing.

So, this book is about how to develop a healthy set of business relationships, a few of which are delivering leads and referrals. It isn't about all the other things business contacts can do for you (other than in passing). It certainly isn't about other ways of marketing and, above all, it isn't about selling.

6 Principles and precepts of networking

Dotted throughout this book are some 'principles' and 'precepts' of networking. The principles are statements of how the world is: for example, 'People remember stories'. The precepts are suggestions: encouragements to behave, think or feel in ways that are useful to you, such as: 'Make the other person more important than you'.

They're principles and precepts, not because they are invariably true (although they probably are). They're principles and precepts because they are worth treating *as if* they are always true.

Anyone can be an excellent and successful networker simply by following these principles and precepts. Indeed, I doubt you even need all of them. Each person is likely to be able to find the selection that is the most useful for them, personally.

Many of the principles and precepts are discussed in section 11. They're summarised in the appendices.

7 Going to a networking event isn't networking

Networking is creating a group of business people whom you know, and hopefully like and trust. If they stay in your group, these people should know, like and trust you, too. Some people like to cast their net wide and include pretty much everyone they've ever met in their group. Others, myself included, like to have a reason for someone being in their group. This makes the group much easier to manage, but you risk missing some interesting people.

As we shall see, a network is a set of *relationships* between you and each person in your group, and between the other people in the group.

Story: Minimal contact

Andrew is a member of a networking club and attends its monthly events. He goes to every event and bumps into Sara at roughly alternate events. They speak for between five and ten minutes each time. After a year, each will have talked for roughly twenty minutes about themselves and their businesses. Given that, each time, neither of them will have seen the other for two months, at least some of their time will be spent catching up with each other. If they discover a mutual passion for skiing, conversations will often focus on that subject.

The amount of useful (that is, business-specific) information that gets imparted, and the extended timescale over which it gets imparted, will mean that at best each of them is 'aware' of the other. And each will have made quite a lot of assumptions (not by any means correct) about the other, too. Being aware of someone isn't enough of a basis on which to warmly recommend them to your best client (or anyone).

You could say, honestly, that, however much the two people enjoyed their chats, their time spent at the event was entirely wasted from a business perspective.

Of course, if Sara's business clears drains and Andrew's rents bridalwear, then there probably isn't a need for them to talk about each other's businesses much. But, even then, neither of them knows who the other person knows (Sara's sister may be thinking of getting married, Andrew's father may run a letting agency with properties on its books needing maintenance, and so on).

NRG Networks runs networking lunches. Martin Davies, one of the co-founders, told me, 'originally people went to events to get introductions. Everything was geared to "I want a referral or customer".' But, this has changed. 'Now I observe the majority of NRG attenders are looking for support. People find the company of likeminded individuals gets them feedback, on big issues and small issues, and they share expertise.' That's why I advocate that people treat the events as places to find people with whom they can develop business relationships outside the events.

Networking events do not provide the time to develop a good networking relationship with another business person, let alone half a dozen people. They are not even designed to do so.

To do that, you need to spend more time in one-to-one meetings: follow-up meetings in which you and one other person systematically discuss your businesses and whether there are any ways each can help the other. Section 16 discusses one-to-one meetings.

Networking is having one-to-one meetings.

The story of Gladys (in **23**) shows that, if you do no one-to-ones, you will struggle to get clients simply by going to networking events.

Networking events are beauty parades at which you decide who you are going to invite to a one-to-one meeting. I say, 'you decide who you are going to invite' rather than 'you decide if you are going to invite anyone', because I always advocate connecting with at least one person: you won't know whether it was worth it until you have done it. If you are new to this game, I seriously suggest inviting *everyone* there, and certainly everyone you meet, to a one-to-one. You just don't know who and what they know, or how you can help them, and it is foolish to 'write off' someone without evidence.

Networking is developing relationships with people who may join your network. You develop relationships by giving enough time to them in one-to-one meetings. So the interesting idea arises that going to a networking event isn't networking. It is the preparatory work you have to do in order to do the networking elsewhere.

8   Networks and networking

Networking is the process of building a network of people. Adding (the right) people to it. Nurturing and developing the relationships between you and them. Facilitating relationships between the people in the network.

Clearly, business networking is doing that for the purpose of obtaining business. It has associated costs in terms of money and time. Because it is a business activity, it is necessary to do it professionally: as well as possible. However, there are hidden dangers. Do too little and you might as well do none at all. Do it poorly (however unintentionally) and you can forget about positive results. It is, therefore, necessary to approach business networking analytically and rationally, as well as from an emotionally intelligent perspective.

It is essential to think of the networks to which you belong outside business before you think about rejecting them. These networks start with family and friends, and could include sports clubs, hobby groups (I used to sing in a choir with 150 other singers, almost all of whom had jobs or businesses), parent groups at school if you have children, local community groups and so on. In some cases, the members of these groups know you better than any of your business contacts.

Story: Church

Rufus was complaining in a class on referral marketing that he didn't have any networks other than a few business contacts. He claimed to lead a sheltered life and, while he acknowledged his family and friends, he couldn't think of any other networks. After some conversation, he revealed that his wife was the secretary of their local church that was particularly active in their community. Bingo! He had to 'admit' he was in a potentially very productive personal network.

A business is a complex interaction of all the relationships between the people in the business, and between them and people in client organisations, suppliers and other stakeholders. Doing more business requires having more relevant people in your networks and having better relationships with them.

9 Leads and prospects

Although there are many reasons for attending networking events, few people will turn their nose up at a nice juicy lead.

But it is important to understand what a lead actually is and how, with a little effort and understanding, one can get much better leads: people who are more likely to be prospective clients. This requires the development of referrers, and these people are discussed in the next topic.

A **prospect** is a prospective client. Usually, you will have met or at least talked to them. Or—and this is the point—someone they know, like and trust has met them, talked to them about you, and pointed them at you. Either way, they know about you, and you know about them.

Most business people, however, define a 'prospect' as someone they think may buy their products or services. A moment's thought tells us that such a vague definition is of no real use. On that basis, with only a little imagination, almost every business is a prospect.

Sometimes the prospect may be a prospective networking partner rather than a client. Such a prospect could be far more valuable than a client.

A **lead** is someone whose name you have been given. If you are lucky, the person giving you the name will have told the lead something about you—but don't count on what they said being accurate or even true, however well intentioned. It's helpful if the person giving you the lead explains to you why they have given you that particular name.

But it is merely the passing of a name from one person to another. Of course, some business people treat the passing of leads more seriously and their leads could be more reliable and desirable but, unless you have had follow-up one-to-one meetings with the people giving the lead, how would you know?

In some cases, a lead can become a prospect (though, inevitably, not all do). In some cases, a prospect can become a client (ditto).

A lead is not a referral. Some people, indeed some networking organisations, like to call leads referrals, because it makes them look more successful. But, calling a lead a referral doesn't make it one.

A referral includes an (un)stated recommendation, based on the referrer's knowledge of the person they are talking about, whereas a lead, however well intentioned, is little more than a name.

10 Referrers and advocates

Some time ago, I had to go to my doctor as I had chronic pain in my right knee. He *referred me* to the X ray department of the local hospital to have the necessary done.

If Helen explains to her colleague, Antony, why he should talk to me professionally, she is referring him to me. For some reason, some people get confused and would say that I was being referred by Helen to Antony. From my point of view, Helen is the *referrer* and Antony is the **referral**.

Anyway, for a lead to be promoted to a referral, the referrer (Helen) has to communicate to Antony if he should talk to me. For that to happen, Helen must not only know about the services I offer, but understand them. She must be able to articulate reasonably accurately to others how these services help my clients in general to solve their problems. Further, there has to be a prior relationship of trust and respect between Helen and Antony, otherwise, when she comes out with her suggestion, he may ignore it. So she also must have some understanding of Antony's business problems so that she can recommend an appropriate person from her network to him.

It is unlikely, if I have only met Helen at a networking event or two, that she will have the knowledge and understanding to do this credibly (just like Andrew and Sara in **7**). A lead is not a referral. Leads come unencumbered with the baggage of recommendation or value.

In the case of my GP, such is the extent of his understanding of local health facilities (and such is my respect for his professionalism) that he only has to say, 'go to this hospital and get an X ray', for me to limp off obediently and do the deed. He doesn't have to explain why, and I certainly don't need to go through a process of examining all the local facilities within limping distance that offer X ray services.

This illustrates an important point that most people are mostly influenced—when deciding whether to employ a service provider—by how persuasive the recommendation was rather than simply on any evaluation of the service provider's credentials, skills, experience and so on (attributes that the prospect often has no real way of evaluating anyway).

This is not at all perverse. It illustrates an important EI point. People are much more willing to listen to, and buy on the suggestion of, someone they know, like and trust, than buy from someone they've never met before *and* whose primary interest is clearly selling their products and services.

As should be immediately apparent, it takes some preparation time for this sort of referring to happen successfully. Each party really does have to understand the other and be able to articulate that understanding at the drop of a hat.

On the whole, you are unlikely to find that someone is willing to be a *continuing* source of referrals for you unless you are willing to reciprocate (though the story at **22** illustrates that it can happen). A successful referral relationship is reciprocal; referrers are partners.

Referrals are usually passive: Angela becomes aware that Dave has an issue and, after some discussion, refers Dave to someone she knows. I use the term **advocacy** to mean a stronger type of referral: one that is active—and proactive. Thelma will go to a networking meeting, say, and promote her advocacy partner, Louise, to the exclusion of promoting herself. This is because she is confident that Louise is going to networking meetings and other events and promoting Thelma, to the exclusion of herself.

11 What is networking, really?

Story: Heaven and hell

A woman who had worked all her life for good causes was granted a strange wish: 'Before I die, let me visit both heaven and hell'. She was whisked off to hell by an angel. To her surprise, she found it was a vast, sumptuous banqueting hall. As far as the eye could see, the tables were piled high with delicious food and drink. Around the tables sat people, but they were miserable and starving.

'Why are they like that?' she asked.

'Look at their spoons,' quoth the angel. She looked and saw the handles were so long that the people couldn't use them to put food in their mouths. 'This is hell!' the woman said. 'Take me away from here!'

So she was taken to heaven. To her amazement, she found herself in an identical, vast banqueting hall. Again, the tables were piled high with delicious food and drink. Again, people sat around the tables—but this time they were happy, joyful and well nourished. She looked at the spoons and was surprised to see they were just the same super-long ones as those in hell. 'But, how can they eat?' she asked.

'In heaven,' said the angel, 'we feed each other.'

In **7**, we saw that networking is developing relationships with people who may join your network. You develop those relationships by giving enough time to them in one-to-one meetings.

It's very important that you work out, and stick to, your own purpose for networking and seek out known outcomes: those that fit you and serve your business well. Of course, if you realise you have made a mistake, or the circumstances of your business change, you should change either your purpose or one or more of the outcomes. There's no point in flogging a dead horse. (We look at purpose and outcomes in **44**.) I believe that:

The most useful purpose of attending a networking event is to find out how you can help others.

Givers gain, as BNI puts it (see **28**). Now, I can help other business people by:

o   finding them clients, or at least warm leads

o   through offers of professional help of one sort or another, *gratis*

o   possibly even by finding them a supplier

o   providing them with some necessary information

o   often it's about giving them useful contacts who can help them.

There are lots of ways of helping. This book prepares the ground for the first of these, giving them good leads and referrals through a mutual arrangement in which you can reasonably expect them to be giving you good leads and referrals.

Given that all of these activities are firmly situated in the business world—I'm not suggesting offering to help them plaster their spare bedroom!—the outcomes are that people have a first-hand experience of what you do and whether you can do it competently.

It is vital to have people in your network who have this basic insight into, and understanding of, *your competence as a business person*. This is *not* the same as having an understanding of your competence in whatever goods and services you actually deliver (accountancy, coaching, clearing drains, hiring wedding dresses and so on) but it is essential for your credibility and if people are to trust you. They get this insight through one-to-ones.

People who have that insight into you as a business person are halfway to becoming valuable business partners before you even start the process (see **41**).

3 Some misconceptions rubbished

12 Introduction

From the behaviour cycle model (described in **31**), we know that our behaviour is driven by our feelings and our beliefs. To be confident of doing things differently (and consistently differently), we need to change our feelings or our beliefs or both. In this section, I talk about a dozen unhelpful beliefs that it would be worth ridding yourself of (if you hold them). Apologies if some of these were cherished, but I assure you that there are alternatives that will serve you a lot better.

It's well worth distinguishing between holding a belief and needing to hold a belief. We hold beliefs to support our world view and, as our world view is part of ourselves, we often resist changing those beliefs, because that calls into question our beliefs about ourselves. Really, it is *needing* to hold the belief that is the problem. The unwanted *effects* of holding the beliefs become a problem, not the beliefs themselves (see the metaphor of keys, **91**).

Rather than trying to replace a belief that X is true with a belief that not-X is true, the best thing to do is to stop needing to hold *any* belief about X. You don't need to think about any new beliefs for the time being. Just be curious about what would happen if you went for a week, a month, a year without any beliefs about X.

If you believe that people will be bored by what you have to say as a result of dropping all these negative, restricting beliefs, adopt an investigative approach: find out if the belief that they're bored is true. Be curious. Be curious about whether they really are bored, or you just think they are bored. Or, maybe, it is you who are bored.

Later, you can strengthen this technique by replacing your unwanted beliefs—not with their opposite, but simply with new beliefs. You can then resolve to be curious about what will happen when you hold and practise these new beliefs. Section 11 discusses some beliefs you will probably find are more useful to hold.

13 'Networking events are opportunities to sell to the room'

Selling to the room is actually quite rare.

> *Story: Grabbing the lapels*
>
> *I was aware of a mild commotion in the room near me before Ethan descended on me. I was chatting to a fellow networker when he butted into my little group and apparently picked on the first person to hand. Almost literally grabbing them by the lapels, he launched into what was presumably his 'elevator pitch' before thrusting his business card at the unwilling listener. Then, with a cheery, 'See you later', which gave them no chance either to ask a question or to complain, he turned his attention to me. The same sequence of events happened before he moved on to his next victim. He was clearly intent on buttonholing everyone in the room.*
>
> *At the time I was a naive networker. Not so naive as to assume that this is what you do at such an event, though.*

In the networking meetings I later ran, such people would have been put on a last warning and told they would have to leave if they ever did it again. Attenders hate it, because it is an uninvited and unwanted intrusion. In extremis, it feels like an attack. Organisers hate it, because it reveals their nice event has fractured, if only momentarily, and out has popped a demon of misrule.

Some unreconstructed people still do this because:

○ They think it works—the one client they ever got this way justifying years of irritating large numbers of people, a few of whom may have considered becoming a client if they hadn't been approached in such an 'in your face' way.

○ They think it is what you are supposed to do (a result of inappropriate advice being given in training courses, I suspect).

○ They think their personal charm will conquer all (it won't)—the self-centredness of the exercise ruins that (see **82** on making the other person more important than you).

○ They are running a serious scarcity model and their neediness is showing (see **118**)—people hate neediness in others, it reminds them of just how close they are to it themselves.

Story: Eggs (1)

Rex had an egg business. He understood the folly of trying to sell to the room. Apart from anything else, it would be ridiculous to set up a stall at the event, and he'd already established that there were almost certainly not going to be any potential clients there.

But he did order some little boxes with his contact details printed inside (just room for three eggs) and gave away some eggs.

The results were:

○ He became instantly remembered by everyone there, whether they got the eggs or not.

○ Those who ate their eggs said, 'I say Rex, these eggs are really rather good, don't y'know!' and became, in a mild way, advocates for his products.

○ He was seen to be a giving person (givers gain) and people warmed to him.

He had to be careful, though. He didn't want to create an expectation that he would always be accompanied by a trail *of eggs wherever he went, so he made it clear that this was a one-off that he had no plans to repeat.*

To be continued...

14 'Networking events are places to find clients'

You might find a client at a networking event, but that's an incidental benefit. Statistically, what is the chance that, in a room of thirty people, there is one whose business is just at the point of needing the services you offer? And, of the people in the room, you happen to bump into them and find that out?

Graciously accept your blessings when the universe showers a client on you at a networking event but, rather than embark on the fool's errand of trying to make it happen again, stick to what networking events are good for.

Networking events are good places for finding people who know prospective clients and who may, given enough awareness of you, introduce them to you. Networking events are 'beauty contests' where you eye up who is there and invite several of them to follow-up one-to-one meetings. At these meetings, it's possible that some of them will pass contacts to you in due course.

15 'Something will happen without me doing anything'

As we see later in the story of Gladys and her dog-grooming business (**23**), going to a networking event isn't networking. Networking takes place in the one-to-one meetings you have with people you meet at the events. Should the organiser have pressed this message home more forcefully on Gladys over the year? Possibly. Should Gladys have taken responsibility for her business and, for example, asked him for advice? Probably.

'Something will happen without me doing anything' is not usually a belief that arises from arrogance or stupidity. It arises simply because people haven't given any thought to how it all works.

As this book aims to show, there is a lot you need to do; but it is easy to be rather good at it. But doing nothing is a high-risk strategy.

16 'Networking is something I can do when I haven't anything better in the diary'

Regrettably, this is a very common attitude. It's understandable that someone in a full-time, temporary job believes that he or she can't leave the office for a few hours to go to a networking event. But it's a false belief in my view, or should be. Anyone should be capable of ensuring, at the time the contract is settled, that they can have small amounts of time off, if only to look after their sick moggie.

Almost all clients will understand that someone in that position—typically a consultant, or interim manager of some sort—who wants to skip from one short-term, full-time contract to another will need a little time in office hours to pursue the next job opportunity. But, oddly, the service provider seems to believe they do not have a right to take time off. I wonder how many of them even ask.

Instead, people create a 'feast or famine' cycle. They have no work to go to when one contract is over, and have lost all the momentum generated by their networking before that contract started.

People, like me, who see clients for individual days, or even hours, often don't press for what is actually wholly reasonable. They are reluctant to change the time of a session, even by a few hours, so that they can conduct some networking activity. Personally, I have a maxim that 'clients come first'. But, I have no hesitation in saying to a client who asks for a session on a day I have already committed to a networking event, 'Sorry, I am afraid I have a prior engagement at that time'. Clients understand this. They have 'prior engagements' too. They'll readily accommodate my diary—not least because they know that my requests for time off are not frivolous—just as I accommodate theirs.

What's really behind both the full-time and part-time person's difficulty is an irrational anxiety that, 'if I disappoint the client in any way, they'll sack me, or they won't extend my contract or some other disaster will befall me. And, in some mysterious way, all other potential clients will hear of this and they, too, will never give me any work ever again.'

Of course, none of those thoughts is conscious (let alone true), it's under the surface. But that doesn't mean it doesn't happen. It's a manifestation of the scarcity model so many people run.

17 'Networking events are places to have private meetings'

There are lots of things you can reasonably do at networking events, but having private meetings isn't one of them. The whole point of a networking event should be for the people there to be available to others to meet and get to know. If you make yourself unavailable for this process, you are not playing the game. Even if you don't accept that the purpose of attending a networking event is to help others, you should at least offer others the chance to see if they can help you.

Of course, if across the crowded room you suddenly see Jasmine, a particularly successful client of some years back, you should go up to her, greet her and spend a couple of minutes catching up. But, after that, have a longer meeting at a later date to give both of you the time and space you may need.

18 'If I don't reply "anyone" when asked who my potential clients are, I will lose work'

This is another manifestation of the scarcity model (see 32). In truth, if you ask me what I do and I say, 'Well, really, I can do anything for anybody', that leaves you floundering. I am so concerned that I don't miss out anything that you could conceivably be interested in that I try to make the answer as all-encompassing as possible. Unfortunately, it doesn't say anything useful.

Story: Class

Graham was attending a training session in how to behave at networking events. It was covering exactly this subject (which is a prevalent one). The students were asked to pretend they were all at a networking event and each student had to say something precise about what they did. Graham chose to say 'I specialise in helping people in the IT industry deal with stress', which indeed was one of the things he did. As the students practised mingling and replying to the question, 'What do you do?', he found that students were moving out of role play and asking, for real, 'That's interesting, I don't work in IT, but my business is stressed. Could you help us?' and 'Well, we're not stressed, but we are an IT firm and we do have some issues'.

Give people something specific and then trust that they are as intelligent as you. They can extrapolate from something that is of little interest to something else that is more so. The worst that can happen is that they ask something like, 'Well, we're stressed, but it's because we need a hitman to take out some dudes. Are you, perchance, such a person?' (Even then, it is permissible to say, 'See me afterwards and I'll give you Fat Tony's card'.)

Give them something vague and catch-all and they will flounder.

19 'I have to have a "unique selling proposition"'

The concept of a 'unique selling proposition' (USP) is still a widespread idea. It is based on the ludicrous premise that there's something about your service or product that not a single one of your 'competitors' has—and that this unique thing will be the one thing (the only thing) that will convince prospective clients to engage you.

Story: Graphic designer

A few years ago, I needed a graphic designer to produce new designs for my stationery, website and so on.

*You won't be remotely surprised that what I **didn't** do was:*

I didn't compile a lengthy list of graphic designers, and interrogate each one of them to establish the degree of difference between them and all other graphic designers on the planet (not just those on my list). This so that I could then confidently choose the one who was most different, knowing that, precisely and solely because they were the most different from all the others, they would be able to do the best possible job for me.

Rightly, you would think I would have been stark staring mad to do this and no-one, in the history of business, ever has done this.

What I did, which is what everyone does, was to speak to a business associate, Lesley, whom I know well and whose knowledge and judgement I trust. I asked her, who would she recommend? She gave me a name, Owen. Of course, graphic designers have an advantage. Their websites will instantly give you a good idea of the sort of work they do. I liked Owen's style and, as a result, we had a meeting.

What Owen did then—which is what every business person needs to do if he or she is to win a new client—was to demonstrate that he was able to resolve the design issues I had in a way that I liked. He didn't have to actually do the resolving then and there when I met him. It was as much about his questioning and analytical techniques as about his design skills. Indeed, by this time, it wasn't necessary for him to convince me of his design skills, or his ability to correctly deduce clients' needs: he did it by showing me.

No business needs to be unique, because being unique is of no value to their clients.

No business person needs to believe that they or their business should be unique. Holding such a belief will actively push people away as potential clients. What business people need to be able to do is to demonstrate to other businesses that their business can help those other businesses solve their problems.

Once a business person has found a supplier he or she believes can solve their problem, they are very unlikely to continue the search on the off chance that there's someone better. After all, time is money. Only exceptional circumstances, such as location and cost, are likely to make the person want to carry on looking.

Business people need to let go of their need to be right about having a USP. They need to be willing, at least temporarily, to suspend their beliefs, replacing them with an attitude of curiosity: 'What would it be like if this USP stuff were irrelevant?' I talk about how to go about this in **86**.

Business people never establish the degree of 'uniqueness' of a potential supplier. They buy from people who have been recommended to them by someone else whom they know, like and trust, and who then demonstrates to them that they fit the bill.

20 'I need an "elevator pitch"'

The idea of an 'elevator pitch' is that you get into a lift (elevator) only to discover inside the very person who, if only you could persuade them, would find the urge to help your business irresistible. What do you say in the thirty seconds or so that you have this person's undivided attention before the lift doors open and he or she walks out of your life forever, your entreaties of 'Richard, wait!', or 'Alan, wait!' falling on deaf and increasingly distant ears?

This is obviously a hypothetical concept. And that's one of the reasons I am against elevator pitches when used at networking events. They are not designed for networking events; they are no use in the situations for which they are intended. They are an insult to the people on whom they are inflicted.

The conventional answer says that you have to get across the following:

○ your name

○ your company name

○ the sector(s) your company trades in (or, at least the main ones)

○ the products and services your business offers (or, at least the main ones)

○ the benefits of these products and services to your clients

○ the help you need

○ why you need the help

○ what you need that particular person to do for you

○ the benefits to them of helping you

○ anything else that could be persuasive.

It is certainly an excellent exercise to be able to do all this in thirty seconds. It really forces one to think in a clear and focussed way about one's business; and the hours that are spent in trying to get it down to 29.9 seconds are really not wasted even when one has realised that it is not possible. (I saw a business student almost fit all of this into thirty seconds, by talking very, very fast. Of course, I hadn't remembered a single thing he said a minute later, but have always remembered that he did it. I remember the emotions I had around the experience of listening to him: mostly surprise, to be honest.)

So, the first reason to avoid elevator pitches at networking events is that they are not intended for networking events.

Another reason to avoid them: they can't be done in thirty seconds and, when the inevitable has happened and the pitch has sprawled all over several minutes, the listener feels on the receiving end of a battering.

The third reason they are to be avoided is that they cannot be crafted to the particular circumstance—that is, the networking event—in which they are used.

And the fourth reason is that, however short and however well crafted, they are still relentlessly and exclusively about the teller and not the hapless listener.

However you structure them, elevator pitches are intended to force the speaker onto the presumed benefactor. And people, benefactors or otherwise, don't like people forcing themselves onto them in lifts.

I'm not saying don't speak to presumed benefactors. I'm saying don't make demands before you've even got your foot inside their door. Set up the conversation in a way that is at least a win-win for both parties and, preferably—on what should be only your first encounter—a win for just the benefactor.

What you should do is tell them a story specifically for this, admittedly unlikely, eventuality. The story must be structured in such a way that it *inevitably* prompts the benefactor to say: 'That's interesting, how did you do that?'

As the lift doors open, you say something like 'May I book a meeting at your office to explain?' You then contact the PA and you may well get a meeting.

(I have another good old chew on this bone in **71**.)

21 'I have to worry about "the competition"'

It's true that the prospective purchaser can only spend his or her pound once. But, hoping to differentiate yourself from others who provide similar services is not the way to convince the prospective purchaser to spend their pound with you. Essentially, this tactic makes the transaction about the seller, not the purchaser: the seller's need to make the sale, the seller's need to be right, the seller's need to 'win'. While the seller needs to make the sale, the purchaser needs to have their problem fixed: there is considerable incongruence here.

Unless there really are only a few clients for some extremely niche service such as buffing up *The Spirit of Ecstasy* on the bonnets of Rolls Royce cars, it is likely that, provided you are in the top 50% of suppliers of the services you supply, there is enough work to go round. Better spend your time and money demonstrating to the casual onlooker why you are in this 50%, rather than fretting about what the 'competition' is doing. (The only reason to study the competition is to ensure that whatever they are doing, you do the something different.)

Worrying about the competition takes time, mental energy and possibly resources; it stops you doing something more useful. It is one of a number of unhelpful practices and beliefs that persist. Just because a lot of people do it doesn't make it right, let alone the best approach, but they do give an entirely spurious credibility to the idea.

There was a time when a lot of people believed the sun went round the earth. As a belief it failed the deeper evidence, and its popularity at the time didn't save it from being untrue.

Just because the person being sold to does it themselves doesn't make it the best approach, either, only the most familiar. The experienced business person needs to be able to make it all about the prospective client or customer. Anything else is self-defeating.

22 '"Word-of-mouth marketing" works'

Well, it depends on what you mean by 'word-of-mouth marketing'. The phrase is typically used when A mentions B to C. This is something that is hardly worth dignifying with the term 'lead' when C gets to hear of it. Yet it implies that what is actually going on is a well-managed, thoughtful process, not dissimilar to what I recommend in this book, when nothing of the sort is happening. Word of mouth confers a degree of value to a lead that it isn't capable of bearing.

It is often *not* helpful for Clara just to pass a lead to me, however well meaning she is in doing so. The problem is that the lead, who may or may not come to me interested in whether I can help them, doesn't really know what I do. He or she will have developed all sorts of misconceptions, partly based on what Clara has told them and partly from their own fertile imagination. If I end up talking to this person, I have to carefully discover, undo and repair the misconceptions without damaging any enthusiasm or interest they have in my services.

What I advocate are proper, well-defined, managed business relationships that yield referrals for both parties.

Of course, sometimes you can get away with it, and the following is your actual exception that proves the rule:

Story: Hospital training programme

Diane's job was to talk to employers to encourage them to put their staff, particularly the junior ones, on training courses. There were government grants for this in those days and she was part of a government quango, so had no interest in promoting individual training providers. Her clients were the employers.

One day, I received an email from Diane:

'If you're interested in working in —— hospital, give the training manager a call. If you're not interested, let me know and I'll find someone else.'

Of course, I contacted the training manager and, in due course, my company was awarded a contract to deliver training in EI-related subjects.

When I subsequently asked the training manager why, having presumably researched other providers, he had appointed me (and Diane confirmed this independently), he said: 'She said: "Talk. To. Jeremy. Marchant."' Four words.

However, the full story is rather more detailed:

Diane and I had had a one-to-one after we had met at a networking event. She was sufficiently interested in what I do that we had two further meetings that were almost entirely me talking through various models and techniques I use, and talking generally about EI, a subject in which she was clearly interested. In all, our three meetings ran to five hours.

As I said, Diane did not deliver an eloquent speech to the training manager about my attributes and skills, such as they are, and why I would be a good fit for the hospital's needs. Instead, such was her reputation among her clients that she only had to breathe on someone and it would generally be construed as a recommendation.

However, Diane's recommendation was not some careless aside. She had spent five hours establishing that I was recommendable in certain circumstances, such as this one. The manager, like Diane's other clients, knew that she would have done this homework thoroughly before opening her mouth, thereby relieving them of the obligation to do the research (so I personally don't think the training manager actually looked at any other service providers).

As a postscript it is worth saying that, once my colleague and I had started working with the hospital, I thanked Diane fulsomely for his help in my getting the contract. 'What can I do for you in return?' I asked, knowing that I couldn't get her clients: she had a fixed, known set of clients whom she served. 'Just don't mess it up,' she replied only half-jokingly. For Diane truly traded on her reputation and she needed me to be another piece of evidence that she was able to help her clients.

This is not 'word-of-mouth marketing'. It is a subtle, complex, time-consuming process.

4   It's just about people

23   Not getting the point

Story: Dog grooming

Gladys runs a rather recherché dog-grooming business. She joined a networking organisation but a year later she didn't renew her membership.

One of the organisers of the networking events asked to have an exit interview and she obliged.

'Why are you leaving us?'

'I didn't get any business.'

'How many one-to-ones did you have?'

'None.'

This illustrates well how a problem (no leads) and its apparent cause (she didn't invite anyone to a one-to-one follow-up meeting) is so obviously behavioural that it is a shock to realise that the behaviour is only a symptom of a deeper, non-behavioural problem, as we shall see.

24   Introduction

I must stress again that, although I home in on the 'networking event' as the forum in which you talk about your business, its products and services, and yourself, everything in the book is relevant in whatever context you are talking to others.

Anyway, I asked Sarah Owen why, in her opinion, so many people are reluctant to network. 'They aren't,' she replied. 'Some are, some like it and are keen. Most don't strategise and utilise what is available both in knowledge and their existing networks. As a result they don't act purposefully with a plan so with an erratic approach they achieve erratic results. They usually know it works and don't know why, so they don't know what to do about any problems they encounter.'

One of the subjects I find fascinating to talk about with business people, particularly those who work in or own small businesses, is what they worry about.

To be honest, if they are worried about the financial standing of the business, or about their issues providing a service to a particularly belligerent client, they may need to hire some help. These things have to be worried about and dealt with. But other people can provide the insight and guidance needed to sort them out—either by taking over the tasks needed to resolve the problems, or by teaching the business person how to deal with the problems themselves.

However, third-party suppliers cannot provide:

o   confidence with other people

o   a capacity to relate to others and to form productive business relationships with them

o   help in developing a personality that is resilient to setbacks.

This shows up acutely in the forum of the 'networking event'. These are often only adequately organised by people who are not themselves sure what it is all about. As a result, the novice networker understandably flounders, lacking sufficient of all three of the above. Having dipped their toe in the water once, and not liked it, they resolve not to do so again. Such a pity. Often, they are the ones most likely to refresh such an event. There are a number of points to make:

o   Firstly, it isn't as hard as you think, and the rest of the book shows you how to make it easy and make it work.

o   Secondly, the business sphere is hardly unique in needing adequate personal relationships for success.

○ Thirdly, by 'showing up', by showing the way, you should have others eating out of your hand—because everyone, and sometimes this includes the organisers, is desperate to find out what they should be doing.

25 Being attractive

Think about any group of people. Who are the people you are drawn to?

○ Those people who seem withdrawn, probably reading the list of attenders, or who seem to be actively uninterested in what you are saying? In particular, they venture no questions and don't contribute to a conversation. People probably don't 'rate' them (see section 15).

○ Those who 'play the game' but nothing more? You can't say they don't show willing and participate. However, they rarely go the extra inch, let alone the extra mile. How much the event may be a struggle for them, they do not reveal; but they basically do not show any real enthusiasm.

○ Or the people other people actually like to be around? Their jokes are laughed at (they make jokes in the first place). They show a real interest in you and in other people, to the apparent detriment of promoting themselves. They offer to help and introduce people they know to you if they think those people can help you.

In a word, you and other people at networking events are drawn to people who are *attractive*.

This is nothing to do with their beauty or handsomeness; I have not yet found a link between pulchritude and business acumen. But there is certainly a strong correlation between general attractiveness and business success.

So, how to be attractive? Here are four characteristics of attractive people:

○ They make the other person more important than them— that is, they *think and feel about other people, behave towards other people*, **as if** *they were more important than them.* **This is the 'leadership precept' (see 82). It is a fundamental component of the approach I suggest to you.**

o They seek to understand the other person; they are interested in them.

o They are physically and mentally present.

o They don't insist on being right.

Attractive people have the right *attitude*, by which I mean that they have a useful combination of beliefs and feelings about business, and networking in particular, that helps them and others.

All of this means that attractive people attract people to them. In particular, they attract potential *clients* to them. They do not force themselves on the prospective client. You cannot start being attractive once you have a prospect in your sights if you haven't been attractive all along. People will see straight through it.

For people who feel they aren't attractive to others:

o Firstly, don't be so sure; the British can take modesty to a fault and this isn't the place to be modest. I don't mean you should brag—I mean be yourself. As Marianne Williamson wrote in *Return to Love*:

   Our deepest fear is not that we are inadequate. Our deepest fear is that we are powerful beyond measure. It is our light, not our darkness that most frightens us. We ask ourselves, Who am I to be brilliant, gorgeous, talented, and fabulous? Actually, who are you not to be?

o Secondly, note that, paradoxically, being attractive is not much more than (a) being yourself and (b) being interested in others—in other words, genuineness and openness.

o Thirdly, there's still the advice to 'act as if'. Providing you are doing this with authenticity, then you will find it works. The more you find it works, the less you have to make an effort to do it and the more it comes naturally.

26 Being authentic

This is a tough one. Maybe we all know what it means to be inauthentic, but authenticity? Isn't that just being ourselves? Why would anyone not want to be that? Yet, of course, it is hard for a business person not to overegg the pudding, hard to stop ourselves 'inadvertently' giving the impression that we are more talented or more successful than we really are. Indeed, it is so easy that the first person we convince of this stuff is ourselves.

Inauthenticity is a defence. It is saying that I don't expect people to accept me as I am, so I shall have to be someone else. This flies in the face of our own experience! We all find inauthentic people grating. A useful maxim is:

> The more open we are, the more attractive we are; the more defended we are, the more we are attacked.

27   Connectors and mavens

In his book, *The Tipping Point* (well worth reading), Malcolm Gladwell identifies three types of person whom you might meet at a networking event (and in every other aspect of life): connectors, mavens and 'salesmen'. Most people are none of these three—a rare few people are more than one.

Connectors know a lot of people: they 'link us up with the world... people with a special gift for bringing the world together'. They are 'a handful of people with a truly extraordinary knack... [for] making friends and acquaintances' (Gladwell). Crucially, however, it is not enough that they know a lot of people—they have to really like connecting the right ones together.

Mavens know a lot of stuff. They are 'information specialists', 'people we rely upon to connect us with new information' (Gladwell, again). They accumulate knowledge and understanding and, again crucially, they like to share it with others and know how to do that.

I prefer the word **influencer** to salesman. I am allergic to 'selling', and I feel the term is unnecessarily sex-specific. Gladwell's 'salesmen' are able to persuade others. They have a way of communicating that encourages others to believe them.

The difference between a *connector* and *maven* is this. If a maven recommends a restaurant to ten people they will all go, because the maven is known to be an expert on restaurants. If a connector wants to get ten people to go to a restaurant, he or she will have to tell a hundred people, because they aren't known for knowing about restaurants particularly. However, they do know a hundred people. Influencers stand out because they influence through their communication skills.

In any networking group, it is essential to know who the connectors, mavens and influencers are, and to ensure they know about you and your business. These are the people to seek out when first joining a group, or going to an event. These are people you must have one-to-ones with, and you must ask whom they know who it would be good for you to talk to. (One hopes that the organiser and host are connectors, so start with them.)

28   Givers gain: networking provides a forum for reciprocity

'Givers Gain' is a slogan used by BNI (Business Network International). I am disappointed to read that, according to BNI's website, this means 'If I give you business, you'll want to give me business'. While that may be an expression of the principle that resonates with BNI's members, it does sound rather like an expectation to me, and expectations—as I hope I show (in **48** and, really, throughout the book)—are to be avoided.

I think the idea of givers gaining means, all things being equal, that people who help others freely, without thought of recompense, receive more from others, unsolicited, than those who are parsimonious. It is essentially an expression of the abundance model. Givers are attractive. And, people to whom you have been helpful in the past are more likely to be helpful to you now than people you have never met. It says that just being seen as the sort of decent person who helps others will encourage people to help you.

Unfortunately, some people do keep a mental balance sheet and feel that they are 'in debt' to you because of your previous helpfulness. See the story *Ledger* (**32**) for a true illustration of how this can get out of hand. Worse, they will consider that, if they have helped you, you are now in debt to them.

It is sad that the idea of 'givers gain' is all too often twisted into a sort of 'I'll give to you but only if I know you'll give me something back'. This is, of course, a demand (people don't like demands) and an expression of the scarcity model: 'I can't afford to give you any of my stuff unless I know you'll replace it with something similar or better'. People who are worried about lack in their business tend to be more stressed than those who are comfortable. People who are stressed are less likely to be patient and more likely to make demands of others. In *extremis*, it is a sort of desperation, and definitely not attractive.

29 Stretch zone

It's natural to avoid situations that are stressful or have the potential to be stressful. Of course, one person's stressor—a condition that causes stress—is another's excitement, exhilaration or challenge. I'm concerned here not with what the stressors are but how they are experienced.

In addition to stressors in business—such as deadlines, cashflow problems, difficult clients—it's important to recognise that we create our own stressors. In anticipating or avoiding a stressful situation, such as a meeting, we create a further stressor (the anxiety about the meeting). In these cases, it is neither the thing itself that is the real stressor, nor even the anxiety we have that the something bad *could* happen. The real stressor is the anxiety that, if the bad thing happens, we will not be able to deal with it. This is a belief for which there is rarely any evidence. The stress is entirely self-induced.

While avoiding stress is necessary at a primitive level, that tactic is too black and white. It isn't the case that something is either stressful, and therefore to be avoided, or not stressful. There are degrees. However, the whole idea of 'comfort zone' is so ingrained in our culture that we see anywhere outside our comfort zone as being in a stress zone.

A more useful belief is to imagine a *stretch* zone outside the comfort zone. This is a space where we are challenged, the adrenalin is raised and we get a buzz. We perform better here.

The stress zone only shows up outside this stretch zone. I suggest deliberately aiming to be in the stretch zone for the majority (but not all) of our working time. This will make us more productive, more effective—better at our jobs. And we will enjoy it all more.

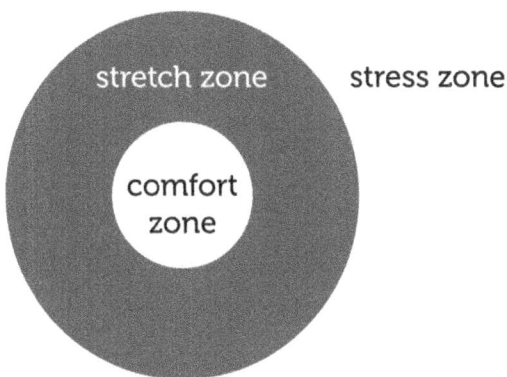

And, the funny thing is, the more we inhabit our stretch zone, the more we get used to it, and the more it becomes absorbed into an expanding comfort zone. So we are able to extend, in turn, the boundary of the stretch zone and successfully rise to new, greater challenges. A colleague told me: 'I like to do things that are "comfortably outside my comfort zone"—challenging, but within my capabilities—nothing too scary. They give me new experiences and make life exciting. But more than that, they expand my comfort zone, allowing me to push out further and further in small manageable steps. Sometimes I look back and am amazed at how far I've come from my old comfort zone. It's an exciting journey.'

As Anaïs Nin wrote:

> Life shrinks or expands according to one's courage.

If all this sounds fanciful, then consider the standard model of stress (on the next page) that shows how performance first increases, but then worsens and worsens as one's reaction to a stressful situation increases. I have mapped the three zones onto this model:

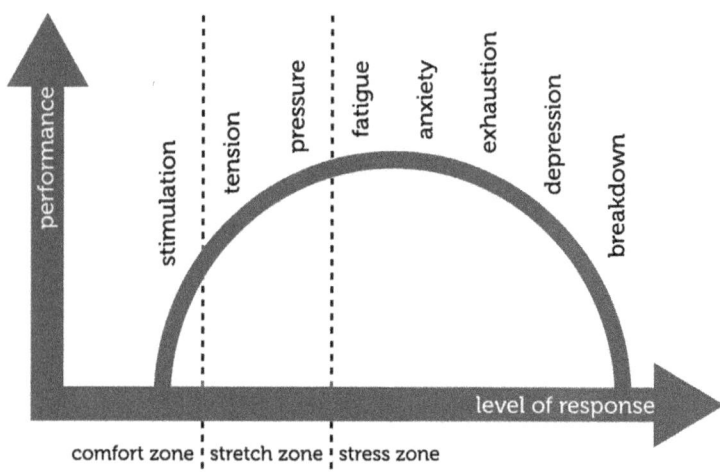

30 Do something different

Story: Alsatians

When I was quite small, my mother let me play out in the street when I was at home (we didn't have cars in those days). We actually lived on a small hill of some fifty houses and I enjoyed walking right to the top and then sailing down on my scooter.

Trouble was, in the house at the top of the road, there lived an Alsatian dog and, occasionally, it got out and prowled the street. I was terrified of it. Unfortunately, at the bottom of the road, there also lived an Alsatian. It too occasionally got out, and I didn't like that one either.

One day, I was playing with my brothers. The dog at the top of the road was out, which I discovered only when I got close to its house. To my acute alarm, it ran towards me and, in my terror, I raced down the hill, no doubt screaming, the dog in hot pursuit.

My mother came out of the house, halfway down the hill, wondering what the fuss was all about. 'It's only a puppy!' she exclaimed, 'I expect it was trying to play with you!', an insight into canine psychology that I did not particularly welcome at that moment.

From that emotionally charged experience, I developed an emotionally charged memory (no doubt unintentionally exaggerating the size of the dog, the loudness of its barking and so on). And from that came quite a phobia of all dogs, and especially Alsatians.

Fast forward fifteen or so years. I was now a barman in the local public house. The manager owned three dogs—Alsatians, as it happens. But they were usually upstairs, so that was alright.

But one evening I had to replenish the crisps, fetching a box from the stockroom immediately behind the bar. The door was always kept open and so it was possible to see into the stockroom from the vantage point where the manager played 'mine host'.

To my horror, one of the Alsatians was 'guarding' the crisp supply, lying on the floor between me and the box I had to fetch. My apprehension must have been visible for I heard the manager's voice behind me saying 'Just walk on it', that is, just keep walking. Assessing rapidly that the humiliation of not fetching the crisps was worse than being torn limb from limb by a crazed dog, I kept walking.

Whereupon the dog sloped off.

It must have happened many times to it.

Now, it came to pass that I was given a special job when the pub shut. Instead of washing the glasses and tidying the place, my job was to take the three Alsatians for a walk in the park opposite the pub. Ordinarily, one might think twice about walking in that park in the dark at that time. But, once I had got the hang of having three Alsatians on leads, all keen for exercise after being shut up in the pub for six or more hours, I felt curiously unafraid.

I recognised that they were more interested in the exercise than they were in sizing up my precise level of anxiety with their doggy brains. Mind you, while one was quite normal, and another rather old, the third was a notorious and violent psychopath. But, you know, he was putty in my hands.

31 The behaviour cycle

The diagram below shows how every person's behaviour is determined by their emotions and feelings, and by their thoughts and beliefs. One cannot act unless one has premises on which to initiate the action, and a context in which to do it. The premises and context are provided by our feelings and emotions, and our thoughts and beliefs. Of course, we are not conscious of all the causes, but that doesn't invalidate the model.

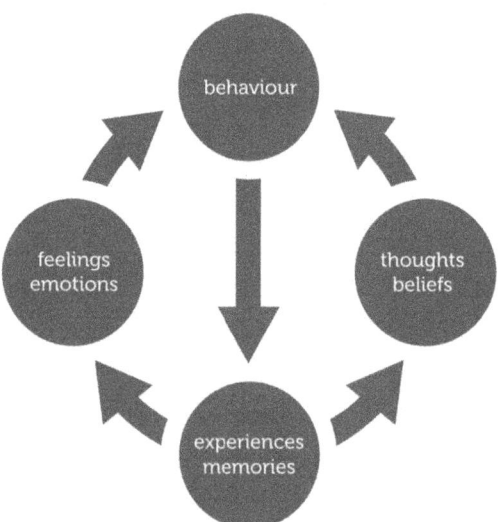

In the case of the true story, *Alsatians*, the initial experiences were of being frightened (feelings and emotions) by the dogs when I was a child. These experiences led to beliefs about dogs in general (they are all dangerous) and feelings about them (I am scared when they are near). This then precipitated behaviours such as avoiding actions.

When I was given a new set of experiences ('walking on' the dog in the pub, taking three Alsatians for exercise), I developed new beliefs (even these dogs are alright, if they have something more than me to occupy them), new emotions (hey! I can handle this!) and therefore I modified my behaviours (far less avoiding action).

So, where we avoid networking events, we usually do so for reasons that have nothing to do with ourselves today, with our business today or with networking events today. The avoidance stems from different events in different situations in our past. In those events we were forced to confront something we were anxious about then and are still anxious about now. After that confrontation, we developed beliefs ('I can't handle walking into a room full of people I don't know') and feelings (specifically the anxiety that, were we to 'walk into a room full of people', we may not be able to control negative responses such as embarrassment, say). Today, recognising the same anxiety of old, we spontaneously attach all the feelings and beliefs we developed then, and that we still carry, to the current event, however inappropriate and irrelevant they are to that event.

It is the anxiety we feel that *we couldn't handle* the embarrassment, the humiliation or whatever that it is important to address, not any imagined anxiety about the experience itself. You can't be anxious about something that isn't happening. But you can be anxious if you believe you can't cope with it when it does happen.

In order to cut through this cycle, we need new experiences, which is exactly the situation I set up for Maggie. She had the new experience of surviving a low-key event sufficiently successfully that she was able to modify her feelings and beliefs about networking. That enabled her to voluntarily attend another networking event, and then another… Each time she went to an event she reinforced the new feelings and beliefs, the old ones began to drop away because they were no longer needed, and she created a virtuous spiral that, no doubt, had benefits in other areas of her business life (such as increased confidence dealing with clients).

Experiences create feelings and beliefs; feelings and beliefs drive behaviour. To change behaviour you have to change feelings and beliefs, often by having new experiences and then creating new memories that are more helpful.

You have to be willing to take that step. Maggie had me, I had the pub owner.

32 Scarcity and abundance models

Scarcity and abundance models are classic examples of the behaviour cycle in action.

A **scarcity model** is a set of consistent beliefs and feelings that there is not enough to go around, and that 'I am not going to get enough of what I need (money, clients, friendship, praise, love…)'. Depressingly common among business people (and not just those in small businesses), it can be toxic.

A business run by someone with a strong scarcity model will be infected by it. Sooner or later, most of the people in the business will be working with that approach. The scarcity model comes to epitomise the business. Members of a business networking organisation run by someone who has a strong scarcity model will become affected by the model.

People who realise they are running the scarcity model should think about how they can reduce its effect. It is, at bottom, just a complex of feelings and beliefs. Choose a different belief, such as 'I have the skills and talents I need to get enough for myself (and my family/business/etc)' or 'There is enough to meet all my needs'.

An **abundance model** is a set of consistent beliefs and feelings that there is enough to go around and that it isn't necessary to compete with people for what we need (money, clients, friendship, praise, love…). Once again, a business run by someone running a strong abundance model will be infected by it. Sooner or later, many of the people in the business will be working with that approach (though others will insist that their own scarcity models, developed long ago, take precedence).

It is unfortunately true that the scarcity model will beat the abundance model in any contest. It's human nature. So people with abundance models need to nurture them—particularly if they are bosses.

Someone running one of the models is likely to have developed them from the experiences they had in early childhood, and the beliefs he or she formed about those experiences. It's not enough to have been raised in poverty to run a scarcity model. The attitude one's parents had to their situation will be crucial in modulating the experience of not having 'enough'. After all, 'enough' is a relative term and, if a child has enough love, not having 'enough' toys is much less of a problem.

Of course, it would be idle to pretend that there are not millions—billions—of people globally living in real poverty. Scarcity and abundance models are not factual reports of the economic situation that applies to the individual: they represent the *attitude* the individual has to his or her circumstances and expectations.

Story: Ledger

Some years ago, I arranged to have a get together with an accountant. As I recall, he worked in quite a large practice in the south west.

The conversation turned to the concept of 'givers gain': the idea that, if you help others, they will be highly predisposed to help you in return.

At which point, the accountant pulled open one of his desk drawers and retrieved an A4 ledger that he opened. He showed me the two facing pages on which he recorded the value of the work that he had received from others, and the value of work he gave to others. His intention was to ensure that he did not pass to others work of a higher value than he had received.

Whether the fact that the man was an accountant predisposed him to this approach, or whether his cast of mind impelled him to be an accountant, I cannot say.

This wonderful, true story demonstrates the application of the scarcity model, big time. It's a belief that there is not enough to go around—not enough work, not enough money, ultimately, not enough love—'and I'll be damned if I don't get my fair share'.

In thinking he would be out of pocket by passing work of a greater value than he received, he completely failed to recognise the substantial amount of work he would likely have got from people who encountered someone with a rather more giving nature.

33 How the scarcity model affects businesses

Most people running a scarcity model look for some way to acquire what they believe they lack. However, a belief that there isn't enough of it makes this a challenge, so they seek a substitute for what they feel they lack. Outside business, this could be political power, for example.

Overwhelmingly, the unit used to substitute for a lack of something emotional, something deeper, is money. Whether as an employee or as a business owner or director, it is money that becomes the focus of the individual's scarcity model. And this is apparently a good thing—according to Western business culture, the acquisition of money is, per se, a good thing. As Peter Mandelson, the socialist UK business secretary, said in 1998, '[I am] intensely relaxed about people getting filthy rich as long as they pay their taxes'.

It is unsurprising that, if a large number of people are running the same model of life, the model becomes 'true' simply because there is a widespread unspoken collusion in the belief that it is true. They collectively maintain social and business structures that have the happy property of enabling the model to be validated.

So, put simply, a scarcity model often uses money as a substitute for something else in the belief that acquisition of money is an acceptable substitute for the acquisition of that something else.

Well over half of business owners and directors are running a scarcity model of some degree of severity or other. It seems likely that, in those businesses where enough influential people are individually running a scarcity model, the whole business comes to embody such a model.

Those people who may be running an abundance model in such a business are, no doubt, looking on in bemusement, wisely not trying to change the beliefs of anyone else, but suffering, like everyone in the business, from this impoverishment of vision, of energy and of success. There is nothing like a self-fulfilling prophecy.

A scarcity model fosters spurious competition where time, energy and resources are spent competing with imagined threats instead of working towards the success of the business. People's behaviour can be seen to be either exacerbating the effects of the belief in scarcity or endorsing it—people essentially collude subconsciously in keeping a business less than optimally successful in order to 'prove' to themselves the truth of their beliefs that there is not enough work out there.

The trouble is, if a business is running this model, the people in it will find it hard not to communicate these beliefs subconsciously to a networking contact. This can often be experienced by others as neediness or even desperation, both of which are very unattractive. Others are duly put off. Alternatively, someone running a scarcity model can be experienced as making demands—again, off-putting. The fact that both parties are unaware of these communications (because they are subconscious) does not mean they aren't happening.

34 Refusing to change

Why don't some people want to change? I was asked this recently by a colleague. He added, 'And of course, we never truly know what drives the behaviours, unless they tell us'. Well, we know what *sorts* of things drive them: emotions and feelings, and thoughts and beliefs. This is the behaviour cycle, as we have just seen.

And, in truth, we actually know, on the whole, what *sorts* of emotions and what *sorts* of beliefs people use to block change. (If only because they are the same ones we use.)

In his book, *The Examined Life*, psychotherapist Stephen Grosz wrote:

> We resist change. Committing ourselves to a small change, even one that is unmistakably in our best interest, is often more frightening than ignoring a dangerous situation. We are vehemently faithful to

our own view of the world, our story. We want to know what new story we're stepping into before we exit the old one.

The story of Damian (see **86**) illustrates that some people will be willing to sacrifice a very great deal (his business, in that case) rather than change.

I'd rephrase my colleague's question ('Why don't some people want to change?') to 'Why does everybody resist change most or all the time?' It's not enough to talk about people not liking being pushed out of their comfort zone. Not wanting to be pushed out of their comfort zone is just another way of saying people don't like change. 'Comfort zone' is just a metaphorical phrase for 'staying the same, having things like they were before'.

Giuseppe Tomasi di Lampedusa nailed it in his great novel, *The Leopard:*

If we want things to stay as they are, things will have to change.

As we saw in **29**, it helps to see that there is a 'stretch zone' immediately outside the comfort zone before you get to the stress and panic.

When I work with business people about why they're stuck, I talk about 'fear of the next step'. Of course, it's not really fear, it's anxiety. (This is an important point, since fear is an instinct, useful and usually to be welcomed when it arises; whereas anxiety is an emotion and therefore capable of being changed, or at least reduced.)

So, where it becomes clear that a business person accepts that they have to change their behaviour and start networking—or change their approach to the networking they already do— they will benefit hugely if they can address making the change at an emotional level.

And they do this by considering their feelings about making the change in behaviour. They think about the anxieties they may have, the beliefs they might have and ask themselves if they need those anxieties and beliefs any more. They think about what beliefs and emotions it might be more useful to have.

Although, frankly, the easiest thing is to just do it.

Story: The Indiana Jones story

This challenge to the individual is expressed in the well-known scene from the film, Indiana Jones and the last crusade. In it, Dr Jones is standing at the edge of a deep chasm. On the other side is the holy grail, but there appears no way across. Luckily he has a parchment showing an old drawing of a man apparently walking on air. 'This must be a leap of faith,' he says. So he steps out into the chasm only to find a bridge under his feet, and soon the holy grail is in reach.

35 Attitude

Attitude is not a negative word. It's true that you can have a bad attitude towards something; but equally you can have a good attitude towards something, for example business networking. For 'attitude' read 'approach', if you like. How good is your approach to networking? Do you need to approach this work differently?

Attitude is not feelings + beliefs. Attitude is feelings × beliefs.

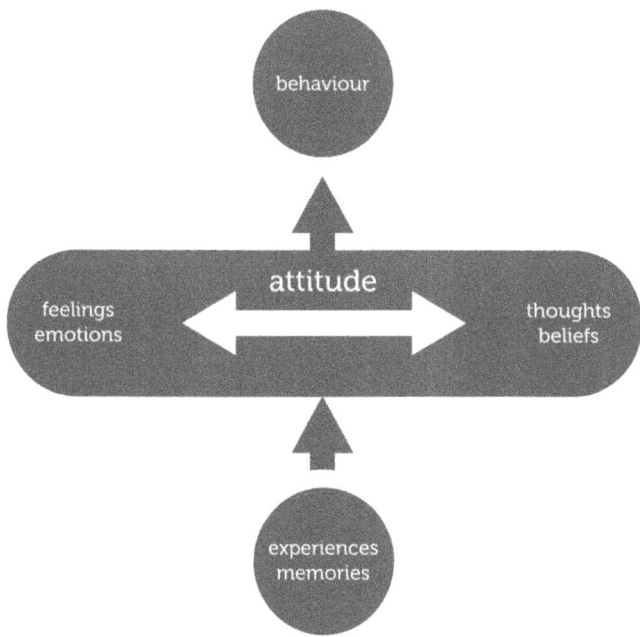

Attitude is passive, whereas approach is usually active. It is the passivity of one's attitudes that we need, at times, to shake ourselves from. Our attitude towards something is the *interaction* of our feelings and emotions about that thing and our thoughts and beliefs about it. It is a third thing.

The statistician George Box said:

> All models are wrong, but some models are useful.

The behaviour cycle model is useful, but it's not accurate in showing the arrows in the way it does. In reality, there should probably be a double-headed arrow between each box and every other box. This may be truer, but it is a lot less helpful, since it loses the important information: it hides the 'prevailing wind'.

So, I show *attitude* as a double-headed arrow between feelings and emotions, and thoughts and beliefs. Attitude is not a sum of those things in isolation to each other. Rather, it arises from the *consequences* of feelings and emotions acting on our thoughts and beliefs, and the *consequences* of thoughts and beliefs acting on our feelings and emotions.

5 It's just about relationships

36 Businesses are just the relationships between people

'Businesses are just people' is a principle shared by many. Of course, the word 'just' is not intended to belittle anyone: it simply means that businesses are *only* people. The principle states that people make up the most important component of a business. This is a values-neutral statement: people may be a business's greatest asset, but they can also be its greatest liability.

It's important to maintain this principle at the forefront of our attention because writers, consultants, advisers, financiers, to say nothing of business people themselves, give disproportionate amounts of resources and time to processes and procedures—to the nuts and bolts—rather than to the people who are actually making it all happen.

Businesses are nothing if not transactional. Not just the commercial transactions between supplier and customer, but also the interpersonal relationships between:

o   each person in the business and each of the others

o   the people in the business and the clients

o the management and staff, considered as groups

o the leaders and everyone else in the business

o people in the business and people in its suppliers and in other businesses (for example at networking events).

So, here is a more useful principle: **Businesses are just the relationships between people**—and between groups of people: directors and staff, marketing team and production, 'the business' and 'clients'. If a business is the sum of the relationships the people in the business have, it follows that networking relationships are *actually part of the* business.

A business no more needs poor-quality relationships with the people its staff meet at networking events than it needs poor-quality relationships with its clients. It's wholly inappropriate to devalue networking relationships because their immediate financial value is low or zero. Firstly, money is not the only measure of the value of a relationship or even an important or useful one; secondly, who knows what the future holds?

It automatically follows that, to be good at networking and building useful business relationships, one has to be good at creating, nurturing and building relationships with other people.

Business people fail to acquire enough (or any) clients through their networking activities primarily because their skills in this area are underdeveloped—not because they don't have those skills.

In fact all businesses that need to provide good customer services, as well as good professional or technical skills, would do well to think that really they are just the sum of their work relationships between people, most of whom are not in the business. And this applies equally to the overwhelming majority of businesses, as well as to the public sector, third-sector organisations and the rest.

37 Why and how relationships with people generate leads (or not)

As Bob Burg and John David Mann wrote in their book, *The Go-Giver*:

All things being equal, people do business with, and refer business to, people they know, like and trust.

Of course, all things are never equal, so perhaps the quotation has a limited application, but Burg and Mann are to be commended for introducing the meme, 'know, like and trust', into the marketing conversation.

'Know, like and trust' is an essential milestone on the road that leads to relationships with people who will refer others to you. Tom is unlikely to mention my name to Jerry with any conviction unless Tom knows, likes and trusts me. There is a reputational issue at stake here. Tom and Jerry have a professional relationship: they know, like and trust each other. Tom is unlikely to want to jeopardise that relationship for my sake. If, on the other hand, Tom and I know, like and trust each other, then, of course, he will happily talk about me.

Humans are emotional and intuitive beings as well as—and, actually, a lot more than—rational ones.

It's telling that the phrase 'know, like and trust' only contains one word you could say was a rational one ('know'). The others are emotions. Networking events are very useful in building a wider, deeper picture of others, beyond a list of their services and clients. That deeper picture has to be acquired somehow: networking events can help, but it is one-to-one follow-ups that provide places for knowing, liking and trusting to grow.

It really is implausible to think that someone is going to risk their reputation with someone who knows, likes and trusts them by referring them to you, whom they have not yet got to know, like or trust.

Story: Accountant

I used to go to breakfast networking events. There would be about twenty people there. I got to really like Reginald, the accountant. On one occasion he brought one of his clients to hear me give a presentation that he, Reginald, had already heard, just because he felt his client would find it useful. Without him explicitly mentioning the subject, I sacked my London accountant and transferred to him.

On the other hand, there was a marketing consultant in the group who, as I got to know him, I wouldn't have trusted with sixpence to go to the shops for some sweeties. I might, of course, have been entirely wrong in that mistrust, but that was what his attitude, as I perceived it, had created in my mind.

38 Relationships

Think about a room full of people, say thirty. It's one of a series of regular networking events; some people will have been to most of the events, for others it's their first time. There are many different sorts of people in the room (capable of being categorised by the services they offer, the businesses they offer them to, the newness of their businesses, the attitudes and approaches of the people in the business and so on).

As soon as a networker starts talking to any of the other 29, he or she is starting the process of forming a relationship with that person. The process will often fizzle out after a few minutes. In other cases, it has the potential to grow and flourish. And then fizzle out. Whatever. The potential of the fledgling relationship can be substantially increased by an understanding of how relationships work and of how to avoid at least some of the pitfalls along the way.

Is it possible to categorise relationships in the same way as it is possible to categorise people? The answer turns out to be yes.

39 Dependence/independence/interdependence

An exceptionally useful way of looking at business relationships follows the dependence/independence/interdependence model developed by Chuck Spezzano of Psychology of Vision.

This model describes the way each person in the relationship relates to the other. This is important information when considering business relationships, wherever they are formed and nourished. In networking, at the point where two business people want to move from mere acquaintance to a more productive relationship, it is worth keeping an eye on this topic (and the next one on power struggle and dead zone).

Essentially, in any type of relationship with another, at any one time, each person may adopt one of three states: dependence, independence and interdependence. I say 'at any one time' because we can flick between those states, often frequently.

These three stages are pretty self-explanatory.

Dependence (which ultimately derives from when we were small children) is an attitude of expecting others to meet our needs. In a business networking context, you can see it in the attitude of Gladys in **23**, who simply expected her membership of the networking association to be sufficient to ensure that others delivered to her a stream of clients. She appeared to be a person who just wanted to sit there and be fed. Of course, this was not necessarily her conscious approach, which, no doubt, was full of networker-y efficiency. But it was going on for her subconsciously.

In using the term **Independence**, I am not referring to self-sufficiency and autonomy, both of which are admirable qualities. Here, independence is specifically an attitude of believing that others will not meet our needs, therefore we have to do it all ourselves. This is the classic business person who believes that 'it's lonely at the top', that 'if you need something to be done, you have to do it yourself'.

Dependent and independent people can both be running a scarcity model. In dependency, people believe they don't have the resources and skills to get work, so they demand others do it for them. In independency, they are reluctant to give away anything they have because they believe, like the accountant in the story *Ledger* (**32**), that they won't get it back.

At this point it becomes clear that many business people, almost all politicians, and many others have chosen to be in an independent position, when, actually, interdependence would be a more useful place to be—see below.

What is interesting is that, in any relationship, if one person is determined to be dependent, it makes it very hard for the other not to become independent—and vice versa—when, again, interdependence would be a more useful place to be. If this sounds implausible, consider your own relationships and those of people you know, whatever the context in which they have happened. And, of course, this is central to how people approach their networking relationships with other people they meet.

The default is for two people to be in a *dependent/independent* relationship. For example, Joe is dependent on Annie for leads, and almost certainly for support in his business, and possibly emotional support personally, all of which is freely given by Annie. Annie, on the other hand is running a story in which 'it's lonely at the top', 'if you want something done, you have to do it yourself', so is actively not interested in being helped (at least on the surface) and doesn't believe Joe could help her if she asked him to (so she doesn't, thereby proving she is right).

A *dependent/independent* relationship can be sustained for lengthy periods. Clearly, while it is the default for most human relationships in whatever sphere they are conducted, it isn't the most useful or productive.

Dependent/dependent relationships tend to drain away quickly into inaction, each person waiting for the other to meet their needs, and moaning when it doesn't happen.

Independent/independent relationships end up in an angry standoff.

Interdependence is where, for the first time, a relationship— whether at work or at home—can become about **us** and not about **me**. It's a stage where the people in the relationship work together for the good of the relationship. In networking, both parties need to be at this stage if their relationship is to really work.

Interdependent people in a business relationship will tend to be willing to put the needs of the other person before their own. As the other person is doing the same thing, both parties benefit equally. Of course, one person can't be interdependent by themselves.

Interdependent/interdependent relationships, which one would hope were the norm, turn out to be not so usual. Usually one or both parties is unwilling to step forward. This is the Indiana Jones syndrome and it occurs here for the same reason as it occurred there (see **34**); that is, fear of the next step. Interdependent relationships are the basis for productive networking relationships. This is the state I am encouraging you to aim for in your business relationships. This is developed further in **82**.

If all of this sounds like an extract from a personal relationships counselling manual, it almost is. There is no obvious way in which relationships between two business people are significantly different from personal relationships between any two people. This is why business relationships between married partners (I mean married to each other) can be extravagantly problematic.

Not actually being in interdependency is the cause of many difficulties, particularly for those who thought they *were* in it (as is also true for personal relationships).

40 Power struggle/dead zone

Dependence, independence and interdependence describe the attitudes of business people in work relationships. 'Power struggle' and 'dead zone' describe the relationship itself. I have to admit that these are rather dramatic terms in a networking context, but they are taken from a wider model about relationships, also developed by Psychology of Vision, and at least they are memorable.

These two stages follow a sometimes brief honeymoon stage. In power struggle, both parties are seeking to have their needs met over those of the other person. In dead zone, they are stuck, not wanting the work relationship to end but unsure how to move it forward. These stages are where both parties in a networking relationship are, unless they are in interdependence. In networking, dead zone, is the usual space to be in, unfortunately.

One important point is that, if people sense they are in either the power struggle or dead zone stage, they may well conclude that the business relationship is over; that it has no chance of continuing—and so they leave it.

Actually, it's rarely true that the relationship is over at that point. It's just that the relationship is stuck and, to get it going, both parties must make an effort. To do this, it is necessary to commit to the relationship working. What does that mean? In truth, it means different things to different people. But one important maxim to follow in this situation is:

Make the relationship more important than anything going on in it.

Until that happens, the relationship is stuck in an unproductive area. The individuals won't learn from the experiences they would have had if they had committed to the relationship (those experiences often being of success). And the likelihood is that the next time they seek to form a positive business relationship with someone else (as opposed to, 'Thanks for the Christmas card'), the same thing will happen again.

Again, if all this has a whiff of marriage guidance that is because people are just people. They form relationships with each other in the same ways whatever the context. The relationships have the same characteristics, whether they are personal ones, or on the sports field, or in politics, in religion or, of course, in business.

41   Awareness/credibility/trustworthiness/partnership

How well do you know another person at a business networking event? Or, indeed, at any business event? Awareness, credibility, trustworthiness and partnership characterise the levels of engagement and interaction that business people have with each other.

It is a basic mistake of those new to networking, and those with a well-developed wish-fulfilment centre, to believe that it's enough that someone is aware of you at a networking event. It isn't.

This model defines how well two people, let's call them Martin and Dave, know each other based on their attendance at networking events and participation in follow-up one-to-ones and other activities.

Martin and Dave used to be unaware of each other. They didn't know each other's names, or what they do or who they work for. Now, at least they are **aware** of each other. Martin could tell someone else—Kim—what Dave did, his name and the name of Dave's business (probably). That's about it. For example, if approached by Kim saying, 'I am desperate to meet an accountant. Do you know if there are any in the room?', Martin could say, 'Well, I think Dave's an accountant, you could try him'. Hardly a sparkling endorsement, but anything more fulsome would be suspect.

You can't be **credible** in someone else's eyes unless they have a reasonable understanding of what you do—and have probably heard a number of stories about your clients and their troubles. That will only happen if you have had at least one one-to-one meeting with each other.

Preferably, if yours is the sort of business that can offer free work without damaging the chances of paid-for work later (for example, a coach, consultant, adviser and so on), give them a free demonstration of what you do by doing something useful for them.

Incidentally, I am dead against offering free services and products to prospects in the hope they will be tempted to pay for more. You just devalue your business. However, offering freebies to show potential *recommenders* what you do is important. It is a powerful way of 'training' them in what you do.

Then, Martin could say when Kim turns up, 'I know Dave's an accountant and he told me some interesting stories about how he was able to help some of his clients. Probably worth talking to him. He's over there.' A much better endorsement, possibly even a referral. Had he tried to overegg the pudding, Martin's own credibility could suffer.

Credibility is obviously needed for A to be willing to refer a colleague to B: after all, who would refer a colleague to someone they did not find credible? But this is a behavioural assessment: how well do they do their job? **Trust** is also needed. The colleague would be reluctant to accept a referral if they knew A didn't trust B, however competent A thinks B is.

Of course, some people are more trusting than others. This is the whole point of including this stage in the model: an untrusting person is less likely to give referrals. Ironically, the colleague may be willing to trust B, but never gets the chance.

Partnership presumes a degree of commitment and trust that cannot be present when two people are only at the awareness or credibility stages.

Here, Martin would firstly say to Kim, 'Tell me some more about what you think you need'. This would ensure that any subsequent introduction is neither a waste of Dave's nor Kim's time. Having had a conversation about this (not just one question and answer), Martin says, 'I think Dave could help you here. As it happens, he's just over there. Why don't I introduce you to him?'

Whereupon Martin then takes Kim by the elbow and guides her towards Dave, who is chatting to some other people. He interrupts them. Dave is pretty sure he knows what is going to happen so he doesn't mind the interruption and, anyway, networking meetings are not places to have private conversations with your client. So, if you are in the 'Dave' position, but are having a private chat and are interrupted by Martin trying to give you a new client, hard luck.

Martin addresses Dave and says, 'May I introduce you to Kim, she tells me X, Y and Z, and I felt you may be able to help her'. X, Y and Z are true things that Kim revealed earlier. Martin then turns to Kim, 'As I was just saying to you, Dave specialises in P, Q and R and I thought he might be able to help you'. P, Q and R are services that Martin has described to Kim.

Each party hears a cogent, plausible reason why they should talk to the other, *addressed to the other person*. At this point Martin should make his excuses and leave.

If Martin and Dave are in a partnership relationship with each other, then theirs is an interdependent/interdependent one.

II   Raising your game

6 Be clear why you are there

42 Prepare well to be successful

It's almost too obvious to say. But I will. Athletes engage in a long process of training in order to compete credibly. They practise regularly to stay fit. Before an event they warm up. Musicians, likewise, undergo many years of training; they practise daily (except my brother!) and also rehearse and warm up before a concert or gig.

A networking event is an event at which you are expected to perform. Or, rather, people will find you a lot more interesting if you hold that belief. Would it not be worth practising beforehand? And engaging in some long-term, but not at all arduous, training in order to get better?

You will be so much more effective if you have worked out in advance why you are there, what you have to do to achieve your goals, and what you have to think, feel and believe in order to achieve those goals.

And, if they have consciously practised, analysing what went well and what went less well at previous events, so much the better.

One of the two pillars of this book is the answer to the question, 'So, I'm doing what you told me, why isn't it working?'

In this section, the reasons it isn't working are that:

o   either you are basically not clear why you are there (that is, which of the sensible reasons to be there you are choosing—and 'getting clients' isn't a sensible reason)

o   or you haven't prepared well enough.

If it still isn't working, please see sections 11 to 15 for many further ideas.

43   Be clear what your purpose and outcomes are

Many businesses are encouraged to define their 'vision' or their 'mission statement'. I find these terms difficult to work with. Few people in a business really talk to each other, day to day, about their vision(s) of the business. They leave that for presentations.

More importantly, it is hard to see how the term 'vision' is useful for working out what you would have to do in order to reach that vision. And, what does your business do when it has reached that vision? Have another vision? In which case, why wasn't this second vision not the first vision?

Mission statements are just as bad. They sound as if they have come off the starship *Enterprise*. But what does 'mission' *really* mean? There are religious meanings (as in 'missionaries'), grandiose meanings (a 'mission to Mars'), trivial meanings ('a specific task'—Merriam Webster); so many meanings.

However, you need to say *something* to people you meet in the course of networking so that they can understand the ethos of your business. I prefer plain words that everyone can understand, and that are directly relevant. So, here are two plain words: 'purpose' and 'outcomes'. They're immensely helpful when talking about your business.

How about **purpose**? What is the purpose of your business? What is the purpose of going to a networking event, or meeting someone afterwards? What is your purpose in having a particular conversation? What is your purpose in reading this book? You get the idea. All human activities have a purpose, it's just a question of working out what it is.

Purpose may be conflated with mission, but I am not at all sure they are the same thing.

Anyway, by using a simple word others may not have encountered in this context, you encourage fresh thinking in them as well as yourself. 'Purpose' is a nice simple word that can carry a surprising amount of varied baggage, as we shall see.

It is essential not to confuse purpose with **outcomes**. Outcomes are events and deliverables that happen as you or your business are achieving its purpose.

Another term for outcomes, often used in planning, is objectives. The objectives of a project, say, are the things we want to have happen as a result of achieving the purpose of the project: they aren't the purpose of the project, nor are they the project itself.

But how often do we answer the question, 'what is the purpose of X?', with 'to achieve outcome Y'? As in, 'What is the purpose of my business?', 'To make money'.

Story: Purpose

Jack's business provides outsourced HR services to SMEs. Jack understood the difference between purpose and outcomes, and he knew that the business's purpose wasn't really to make money or even to have fun. Making money was an outcome, along with the healthy profits, the growth of the business, the fun and the nice cars parked outside.

This business could have decided that achieving one of these outcomes was its purpose. But Jack was willing to entertain an objection from me each time he proposed a new purpose. Each time, I put it to him that, maybe, it wasn't the most helpful purpose. One time, he suggested that the business's purpose was 'to provide high-quality support at least as good as the terms of the contract'. An interesting answer—but is it a good purpose? It certainly could be a valid purpose, but surely it is a description of what the business does. It's the thing they do that, if they do it well, will achieve their purpose.

Jack decided that the purpose of his business was to enable its clients to avoid legal action should they mess up a staff issue. This was the unpleasant situation that his clients were prepared to pay his business to help them avoid.

> *In other words, the purpose of his business was to help its clients solve a problem that they needed to solve.*

If you can define the purpose of your business in terms of a problem or issue that the client has that you help them solve, you have got a useful purpose.

With networking, it may be tempting to say the purpose, obviously, is to solve the problem of not enough clients. That's fine. It would work, but maybe I can persuade you of a better purpose.

You can argue that Jack's clients' avoidance of litigation was also an outcome. My point to Jack was, as a purpose, it was useful, whereas making money wasn't. It pointed the way for him to grow the business: offer more support services in adjacent areas it didn't currently cover. Crucially, it was a very strong marketing proposition (and it was true).

44 Purpose and outcomes model

So, there is a third component to the model: **actions.** The actions are things you do that are designed to achieve the purpose which—if it is achieved—will secure the outcomes.

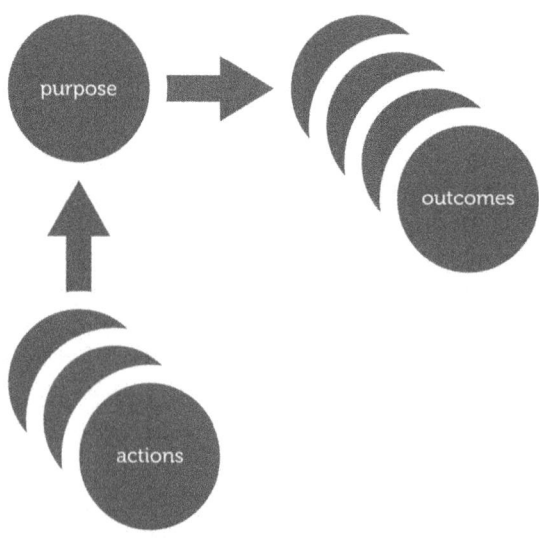

In the case of Jack's business:

o it provided 'high-quality support at least as good as the terms of the contract' to SMEs (the *actions*)...

o ...so that their clients could avoid costly and reputation-damaging litigation (Jack's business's *purpose*)...

o ...that resulted in healthy profits, growth of the business, happy, relaxed clients, nice cars parked outside and so on (the *outcomes*).

It is essential to be clear about the purpose, outcomes and main activities of your business, so you can articulate them clearly in networking and other meetings. After all, a jolly good answer to the question, 'What do you do?'—so often the kiss of death at networking events—could be, 'Well the purpose of my business is X and to achieve that we do Y'.

It is also valuable to talk in these terms to other business people at these events. Many times an innocent, 'So, what's the purpose of your business?', has stopped someone in their tracks. 'I've never thought of it like that before. How interesting.' You've already given them a little present, a new way of looking at something about which their thinking was already stale and too comfortable. And you've shown your way of thinking is novel and vaguely interesting.

It is vital to be clear about the purpose and outcomes of your networking activity, so that you can assess whether what you are actually doing is the most appropriate to achieve your business's purpose and thus deliver its outcomes. Do also be clear, the purpose of your business's networking activities (that several people may be involved with) is not the same as your own purpose in doing the networking.

Story: Eggs (2)

Rex has decided his purpose in networking is to find people who know businesses who buy lots of eggs.

The primary outcome he desires from networking is some introductions to useful people in businesses who buy lots of eggs.

His actions, therefore, in the networking event, are simply to invite people to follow-up one-to-one meetings. He is realistic enough not to make assumptions about the value of such meetings before he has them. One useful tip he says to himself, 'Not only do I not know who this person knows, I don't know who their colleagues, contacts and spouse/partner know either'.

Rex attends networking events because he wants his business to sell more eggs. It's a high-margin product but, precisely because the eggs are expensive, breakfasters are reluctant to buy them. He wasn't making much progress at the events even though he had a box of samples that he was offering to fellow networkers at 10% discount.

Incidentally, the samples idea was a poor one: people don't go to networking events to buy eggs. Had he had the emotional strength to give them away, he might have had a few takers, though.

Anyway, I asked him, why do you go to networking events? That's the same as asking what his purpose is in going to the events.

'To sell eggs?', he ventured tentatively. Well, he had proved to himself that that wasn't working, even at 10% off.

'To find some customers who will buy eggs,' he tried. Well, if he is talking about the person in the street, then a networking event is hardly an efficient way of selling a few eggs— basically using the event for retail purposes.

'To find some trade customers,' he tried again. Shops, but also hotels, pubs, anyone who buys eggs in bulk. That's better. It's a business-to-business concept. But, there aren't many such businesses at the sort of events Rex attends. (Or any, actually.) So, he would have to be pretty lucky not only to find one, but to find one in the egg market at that moment.

Eventually, we got to 'To find some people who may know trade customers'. Now we were getting somewhere.

Selling eggs is an outcome, not a purpose.

Finding retail customers isn't Rex's job, he needs some shops to do that.

Finding trade customers is better, but really it's an outcome masquerading as a purpose. Because, if he sets his purpose as finding people who may know trade customers, as soon *as he achieves that purpose, by definition he has those trade customers—his outcome.*

To be continued…

Once you are happy you've answered the question, 'What is the purpose of your business?', try this exercise: if you answer that the purpose of your business is A, then imagine someone asking you, 'but isn't A *really* an outcome?' We saw the start of this in the story above. Even if you are confident your purpose isn't an outcome, try asking yourself, 'but, if it *were* an outcome, what would the purpose *really* be?'

Then, whatever purpose you come up with, imagine being asked, 'if *that* were actually an outcome as well, what would the purpose *really* be?' And so on. You should be able to get down two or three layers.

A purpose is a tool that helps you decide what more actions or what different actions you could take in order to get more or different outcomes. If the purpose of your business is to have nice shiny cars, you are none the wiser when it comes to growing and developing the business (see Jack's story in **43**).

Your purpose in attending a meeting, say a networking event, may be different from other people's purposes in attending. If this isn't acknowledged, conversations are likely to be unfocussed, somewhat discursive and even pointless. In fact, this is one of the main reasons why many people report dissatisfaction with the networking events they attend. No-one really knows why they are there!

This is not complicated, it's just a bit messy. And that's a very good reason for being crystal clear about purpose and outcomes.

Purpose and outcomes go together like a horse and carriage: there is no point in networking in a way that cannot achieve the outcomes you believe are needed. On the other hand, if your time and resources restrict you to only so much networking, then you need to be confident that the outcomes you will get will be sufficient. You'll want to think carefully about what networking you do, and how you do it, in order to maximise your outcomes from it.

45 Any meeting, conversation, business, job, etc can have only one purpose

If it looks as if there are two purposes to something (whether a business, or going to a networking event or life), then one of three things must be the case:

o the purposes are in fact the same thing, but expressed differently—so find a wording that covers both

o one purpose is a subset, a special case, of the other, so again there is only really one purpose—find a way of incorporating the special case within the general (or just ignore it!)

o there are two purposes. In this case the business, or whatever, is literally at cross-purposes. It is like a sled being pulled by two teams of huskies, each team moving in a different direction. At best, progress is slow and, in all probability, the business is hampered by confusion, missed goals and stagnation.

So, the 'better purpose' of networking, mentioned in 43, is to help others. This will result in others helping you.

46 Be clear what you are going to talk about

Most people, in my experience of many hundreds of networking events, usually talk about two things when they talk about their business:

o the products and services they offer

o the benefits of those services.

I suggest that these aren't the best things to talk about.

It is a common misconception that, before purchasing, business people assess the benefits of the product or service they are considering buying, that they weigh these against the benefits of rival products and services, and then make a decision based on a mixture of cost and benefit. Why this misconception is so common is a mystery, given that most business people know they don't do this themselves.

For a start, isn't it more important to establish that the service meets the presumed need?

Of course cost, by itself, comes into play, though people often do not buy the cheapest. But benefits? if I say the benefit of my widget is that it is an exceptionally attractive blue colour, the punter has to work out for themselves just how this blueness is relevant to his or her business, however convinced I appear to be that this is a benefit for them.

It's pointless for vendors to guess what benefits their prospective clients might find attractive, particularly if the vendor has a shrewd idea that the prospective clients don't know.

It's also pointless for vendors to guess what benefits their prospective clients might find attractive when the prospect knows that the vendor has no idea what he or she will find attractive, and the vendor is just making him or herself look foolish.

It is often hard to associate a particular benefit, as expressed in the vendor's terms, with a particular need, as expressed in the prospect's terms. It is disingenuous bordering on the deceitful for vendors to suggest to uninformed prospects that the 'benefits' that the vendor sees in their products will axiomatically be beneficial to the prospect.

This is important when talking about your business and its products and services at networking events. If the person you are talking to doesn't understand why their business needs the 'benefits' you proclaim, you are not going anywhere. Far more importantly, if the person doesn't understand why these benefits might be needed by their contacts, he or she is unlikely to raise the subject with those contacts (if only to avoid looking a fool when asked 'So, how do these benefits solve my problems?').

Businesses buy the solutions to their problems, not benefits. More precisely, they buy the product or service that will help them solve their problem. At least, they would be advised to adopt that policy.

I need my accountant, Giles, to take away all the hassle. I am not good with accounts and I need Giles to just get on with it. If I were to do my own accounts and submit my own return, it is almost certain I would make mistakes, some of which the

Revenue may not look kindly upon. At best, it would take a lot of my time. Until such time as he puts a foot seriously wrong, Giles has my business.

(I should explain that Giles is my accountant because he and his business partner took over an accountancy firm when the owner retired; the owner was the very accountant, Reginald, in the story in **37**, which just goes to show that occasionally you can pick up a client from among the group you network with, as Reginald did with me.)

So, rather than benefits, talk about the *problems* your clients have that your products and services have helped them solve.

I am not a great fan of going into products and services either. In most cases, you can't be sure that all your listeners actually understand what your products or services are: as with me and whatever Giles does to keep the taxman off my back. You can't be sure that your products or services interest all your audience: even if you are the local Porsche agent, only some of your audience will be bothered.

However, if you talk for a minute or so to me about how renting a Porsche from you will solve a problem my business has which renting a Ford Focus will solve less well, I am at least curious. If only because I may mention this to any of my contacts who are thinking about replacing a car, even if I am not.

Rather than talking about products and services themselves, talk about how those products and services help your clients solve their problems.

But, in a networking event, to do that you have to know what the problems are of the contacts of the person you are talking to, none of whom you have ever met. (After all, you want that person to talk about you to their contacts.) Obviously, not possible. What you *can* do, though, is tell a story or two about the sort of problems these contacts may have or probably have.

People will forgive you for not being specific if they know a story is coming.

If you want to be memorable, use *stories* to explain how your products and services help your clients solve their problems. I cover this essential subject in section 8. People remember stories remarkably better than they remember an exposition about services. Why is this? Because, frankly, the stories are interesting and the detailed exposition isn't.

Having a good story to tell should actually determine which services you choose to talk about when networking. The listener will remember you if you tell a good story about something they're not interested in—in exactly the way that I remembered Gareth the financial adviser when he told his story (in **67**). If you just go on about something that you are interested in then, with the best will in the world, they will have forgotten you as soon as something more interesting turns up, such as breakfast.

Be remembered. I will go out on a limb. In the next topic, I talk about intentions. You should set an intention to be remembered after you've attended a networking event. End of.

There is absolutely no purpose in going to an event if no-one remembers you afterwards! I am not saying, be remembered for anything, such as turning up in a clown's suit. That may be a good idea if you were in the circus business, of course, particularly if the alternative was bringing a few lions along. I am saying, be remembered for something interesting (preferably), or at least relevant to others. Something intriguing, or even compelling—like a story. Something amusing. Something that will encourage people to say 'Yes, I remember you'. If you invite them to have a one-to-one (which I urge you to do), they reply, 'That would be great'.

47 Be clear about your intentions

An intention is not the same as a purpose or an outcome. Although this may seem like splitting hairs, the differences are real and useful.

44 looked at purposes and outcomes. However, Jack's own purpose when he was at a networking meeting was different to that of his business. Jack's networking purpose was to help people he encountered at the events (this would then generate useful meetings with people who may know clients, or even be prospective clients).

In order to ensure he spoke to enough people at an event, Jack set an intention that, at a particular meeting, he would speak to three people he hadn't spoken to before. That was his target. It wasn't an expectation, a demand on himself. It was simply a goal that he used to ensure that he kept moving around the room, not getting sidetracked, and to ensure that, over the long term, he spoke to enough new people.

(Of course, he set another intention: to be remembered.)

To make the distinctions:

o   purpose and outcomes are long term; intentions can be one-off

o   purpose and outcomes can relate to a business, and to an individual; intentions are only ever personal, and relate to specific events or situations

o   purposes can be generalised; intentions have to be specific—they're action targets.

48   Be clear about your expectations

Broadly there are four categories of things of which we have expectations:

o   experiences—a holiday, a tv series

o   objects—for example, a television

o   other people

o   ourselves.

Of course, some things, like family holidays, can be a letdown for all four reasons.

Looking at the third and fourth categories (that is, all the situations where we tend to have expectations of people), the question is, how does someone of whom we have expectations feel about this?

Most people experience an expectation as a demand. If a child has expectations, most adults can handle the implied demands. But, when it comes to adults, it can be much harder. What is it like to be on the receiving end of an expectation?

Firstly, we believe the expectation we perceive the other person has of us is unreasonable or unwarranted. Secondly, while we hear 'expectations' consciously, subconsciously we pick up the demand. We aren't sure why we find the expectation galling, but we do. This explains why having expectations of ourselves is so unhelpful.

Many people feel they need to stay in a dependent position with respect to other people—that is, they need to make other people responsible for meeting their needs. Paradoxically (as it appears), they often do so by being very giving.

But it isn't true giving. It is **giving in order to get**. Often when we give, whether it is a referral to a business person, or a sweet to a child, we have an expectation that we will get something back—a referral in return, or the love of the child. Often, that expectation is unconscious and, because it is unconscious, we are not aware of it at the time. We might even deny it is there.

However, expectations—unconscious or not—*are* experienced as demands, and people don't like demands being made of them. So they don't reciprocate and the giver ends up frustrated and empty-handed.

One simple way of dealing with the disappointment that our failed expectations deliver is to follow the maxim, as best we can:

> *Deal with the world as it is, not as we want it to be.*

All the time we pretend to ourselves that we really are such giving people, and neglect to examine what is in the feedback we receive, we will experience a mismatch between what we think is the case and what we experience.

More practically, the task is to discover how to deal with each of our individual expectations. The best way of doing this is to let go of our need that things (or people) are the way we want them to be. Simply: let go of those expectations.

On the whole, people don't like the idea of not having expectations—partly because it is unusual. Most people say that not having any expectations means expecting nothing will happen. But, **expecting nothing will happen is an expectation.**

I give the example of letting go of a bunch of keys, as a metaphor for letting go of expectations, in **91**. It is the *attachment* to the expectation—or the need—that is the problem, not the expectation itself.

What to replace the expectation with?

a **Curiosity**. Just be curious what will happen if you don't have an expectation that someone will be a certain way and see how they respond. Or that a situation will be a certain way, or that certain things will happen. Or accept that circumstances will turn out the way they were always going to, irrespective of your demands and expectations.

b **Intention**. It's fine to intend that some event will turn out the way you want it to. *Intending* to hit a golf ball into a hole isn't expecting (demanding) that it will. Intention is about personal mindset: it's about what you are going to do, whereas expectations are about what happens when you've done it.

49 Be clear about what you need

Most people don't like being 'sold to'. Most people don't like their car dealer calling out of the blue effectively demanding that they buy a new car, as happened to me this morning. As I explained to the caller, when I need a new car, I may contact them, or I may contact someone else. Actually, the more pushy they are the less likely I am to call them.

What makes it worse is that I have told them, from time to time over the years, that I do not welcome their sales calls. And they still do it, because their need to make a sale at that moment is more important to them than my need not to be harassed. Yet, if they were to spend more time attending to my needs and less to theirs, paradoxically, they would be more successful. Because, in the long run, I am most likely to buy a car from them (when I am ready) if they demonstrate *consistently* that they have my interests at heart.

Story: Laptops

While making me a cup of coffee, one of my colleagues was regaling me with his experiences at a certain computer retailer.

He had made it clear to the salesman that he wanted to buy just two laptops for his daughters—nothing else. So, when the salesman attempted to sell him some ancillary software products, he politely declined. Moments later, the salesman had a second go, and my client explained firmly that he only wanted to buy two laptops, so please stop trying to sell him other things. Undaunted, the salesman carried on pitching the software and my client felt it necessary to threaten to walk out if the salesman didn't stop.

Amazingly, the salesman still persisted—so my client turned on his heel and left, the laptops not bought. He walked straight into a department store nearby and explained very clearly that all he required was two laptops. This store has a much smaller range than the computer shop, yet the second salesman was able to suggest a model to my client who then bought two of them. The nice twist in the tail of this story is that, at the till, this salesman just happened to mention that my client's daughters would benefit from some software packages that were available. He duly bought a couple.

How was it that the second salesman succeeded where the first failed? The key point is the intent behind both salesmen's behaviour. The first salesman's remuneration is based on performance defined by value of sales personally achieved, so the salesman has a clear interest in maximising the value of the sales he makes, as evidenced by his persistence. The second person is an employee on a salary and has no financial interest in whether the client buys or not.

Of course, as a member of staff, he has a wider interest in the success of the business and knows that that success is based at least as much on customer service as it is on price. He also has a more genuine concern that the buyer buys the right thing. He believed my client would find knowledge of the extra product of value. In short, the first salesman was pushing the extra products for his benefit; the second was doing so for his customer's benefit.

Of course, the first salesman believed that everything he said was of value to the customer. It was. But he said it out of self-interest; the benefit to the customer was secondary (it was an outcome, not the purpose of the conversation). And my client picked up this self-interest. Human beings are very good at picking up subconscious communication around needs.

The salesman would never say 'I demand you buy this extra item', but that is the message the customer picked up. We don't like demands being made on us. We resist them. The louder the demand, the more we resist. Hence my client walked out when the demands became tiresome.

Because the second salesman wasn't making an unconscious demand—he was genuinely and simply being helpful—my client was convinced of the reasonableness of the proposition to buy the additional items.

I've laboured the point because it's clear so often that people make demands at networking events that are annoying and thus unrequited. They are therefore poor networkers because they are not putting the needs of other networkers before their own.

You will know that, in a networking event, you are being demanding if you feel any sense of disappointment when the other person moves on, without closing the conversation about your needs.

It's a tough one to eradicate completely, but the idea is to pull people to you, rather than push yourself onto them. The easiest way to pull them to you is to be interested in them and their business at the expense of telling them about you and your business. Be aware of the dynamics of the situation and set an intention that you won't push.

50 Be clear about your target markets

Elsewhere, I advise that having a good story to tell will determine which services you choose to tell stories about. If you don't have a good story about a particular product or service, it's better to tell a good story about something else than a poor story about what you want to promote. Poor stories will just make your listeners question why they are listening to you.

At a strategic level, choice of target markets must partially be determined by what you can coherently and compellingly talk about.

Story: Eggs (3)

Rex decided that his target market was the hospitality sector and not, for example, the retail trade. He decided, based on a little research, that there were plenty of hotels, restaurants, bars and so on that proclaimed their provision of high-quality food. In a sense, these businesses could not but show an interest.

Also the hospitality sector is quite well defined, so there would be no difficulty in identifying trade bodies with whom he might work.

In the retail sector, Rex's products would be on the shelf alongside 37 other brands of eggs; he couldn't rely on shops promoting the eggs well or at all (unless he paid them to do it). Better to approach this sector when he could demonstrate good sales elsewhere.

To be continued…

As we saw in **18**, trying to cover all the bases, whether in terms of what you offer or to whom you offer it, is not a good idea. Although it seems like this would maximise the reception of your message and you couldn't possibly miss anyone out, in fact all that happens is that either your message is hopelessly detailed or it's hopelessly vague, or both, and no-one remembers anything you said. And, if no-one remembers what you say, why did you go to the event?

So, for the purposes of a networking event, choose a small number of sectors (such as one) in which you want to be seen to be working. Only depart from it if you find yourself talking to someone who has declared a huge affinity with a sector not on your shortlist. Tailor your stories to them.

51 Be clear about who you want to talk to

Now you know which services and products you want to talk about, and which market sectors you want to refer to, how do you help the person you are talking to give you a helpful response? If you want to promote marketing services to the coaching sector (almost all one-person bands), your tactics need to be different from those for promoting specialist technical equipment to the health sector. Every sector is structured differently, so your approach must always be tailored to the specific sector in which you are interested.

You need to be very clear whether you are looking for clients or for referrers. Bearing in mind that the person you are talking to at a networking event or one-to-one is very unlikely to become a client, the people you are interested in meeting fall into two categories:

o   people who have the authority to commission work (this could be the sole trader on the one hand or a procurement executive in the NHS on the other)

o   influencers, that is, people who can influence the people in authority.

Story: Squash partner

I was interested in coaching in the public sector. I asked a networking colleague, John, if he knew anyone at senior management level locally. He gave me the name of someone who actually turned out to be the wife of someone he played squash with. He had never met her, so my contact with this person, let's call her Jill, was rather cooler than I would have liked. But I gave her a call and, luckily, she was interested in what I had to say. So much so that she invited me to a meeting that we duly had. As a result of that, she referred me to the workforce development director of this particular department, and he agreed to see me. Within forty minutes of meeting me for the first time, he had given me a job.

You can guarantee that, most of the time, the leads who turn into clients will have arrived in your world by this sort of circuitous route. Note that at no time was anything so sophisticated as referring going on: my networking contact didn't know Jill; Jill didn't have anything like enough information from me to persuade the director (but she probably communicated to him her intuitive response to our meeting); the PA certainly knew almost nothing before she obtained his consent to the meeting.

You are likely to find referrers among businesses that offer similar services to yours—services that are *adjacent* to yours. You need referrers to be convincing when they talk to other people about you. If they are likely to have some knowledge of what you do because it is close to what they do, they will be more credible in their contacts' eyes.

There are always exceptions that prove the rule but, on the whole, wildly differing businesses are not going to know much about each other. The exception to this is where business person A has been a client of business person B. Then, we have the best possible conditions for a referral.

Story: Team development

Barbara and her partner run a business offering personal and team development workshops on the farm. You cannot fail to remember what Barbara's business does if you have had an experience of its services—which necessitates interacting with a variety of bovine and ovine beasts (it not always being apparent who is chasing who). This is why she offers taster events for networking groups.

Two photographers will struggle to give referrals to each other unless there is a very clear distinction between the types of photography they do (for example, commercial and domestic), in which case it could be a marriage made in heaven if each respects and values the work of the other.

Photographers, graphic designers and copywriters all need to seek out website developers. Website developers should be suggesting to their clients that they employ professionals in these areas, so they are a natural source of work for the others. And commercial website development is so widespread a requirement that it is inconceivable that photographers, graphic designers and copywriters don't have clients, and don't know people, in need of a better website—if only because, on the whole, all small businesses need better websites.

Whether looking for clients or for referrers, umbrella organisations constitute a worthwhile group to explore, particularly for market sectors that are fragmented into a large number of small operations.

An **umbrella organisation** is simply an organisation whose members are businesses and/or business people:

o   chambers of commerce, boards of trade and the rest

o   trade bodies, usually organised by profession

o   networking organisations.

Rather more nebulous, there are:

o   colleges and universities that sell to businesses (one would hope that the business school attached to each university was particularly clued up about this—sadly, this cannot be guaranteed)

o   miscellaneous, and usually short-lived, government-created quangos, some of which have funds to give to businesses

o   Rotary clubs and similar (though I cannot guarantee you won't have to undergo some sort of initiation ceremony).

In all cases, the technique is the same. Find out who manages the organisation, or its local branches, and approach them with a genuinely beneficial offer. This could be some free workshops for members; it might be some free work with the people who run the organisation in order to improve it. As usual, it is easier for some businesses to do this than others. Here, it's about being imaginative.

Develop a relationship with them in one-to-one meetings so that, once you have convinced the manager(s) that you are competent enough to deliver these services, they will be more likely to recommend you to their members.

Chambers of commerce may require you to be a member (and why wouldn't you join?) and then they get sniffy about promoting one member's services above others—the key there is to show that there are no members who do *exactly* what you do, so there is no-one to be offended. However, I am talking about referrals, not blanket promotion. You are developing relationships with people who know individual contacts. To a degree, it depends how lucky you are.

52   Be clear, before you attend the event, about what you are going to do after it

After a networking event, you need to have time to follow up the conversations you have had there. Depending on your business's needs, who was at the event, your availability and how long you have been networking (in general and at that particular series of events), you'll need to do some or all the following:

a Decide who of the people you met you are going to invite to a one-to-one. The answer cannot be none of them, because that would mean you are not networking (networking being the development of relationships, not the going to the events).

b Invite each of them to a one-to-one meeting (section 16).

c Update your contacts database; add not just those you invite to a one-to-one, but also other people of interest.

d When people decline your invitation, record that too, unless they have turned you down with such hostility you would rather never speak to them again. (Many declines are really, 'not now, I am too busy, but maybe later'.)

This means you need to think about what type of person you are going to aim to meet, what you are going to say to them and what outcomes you seek, before you walk through the door.

7 You need a portfolio

53 Creating a portfolio

Your portfolio is vital. You need it whether you're actively networking or you just find yourself talking to someone. It is an all-purpose set of resources that is always useful, though it may need supplementing with specific materials for each particular event and conversation, particularly if you are new to the game.

Your portfolio is more virtual than something you can hold in your hand. Primarily, it consists of stories about clients, descriptions of your business and your products and services, anecdotes, jokes, conversation starters, stuff about the local business community and possibly the local and national news of the day. The more of this material you have at your fingertips, the more impressive you will be. People always respond to someone who is able to communicate with them easily and effectively.

Your portfolio is primarily in your memory, though you may have a few diagrams and pictures in your briefcase. If your business makes and sells products, then pictures of them, or even the products themselves, are always appropriate. However, pictures of your factory or your secretary are unlikely to be useful.

Nothing kills a conversation more quickly than saying 'I have a presentation. May I show it to you?' and then ignoring the typically British strangulated objection, 'Oh, I would really rather you didn't'. Such presentations are lectures and, when they are nothing but printed-off PowerPoint slides, a positive insult to the person you are talking to (because, by being prepared in advance, the slides couldn't possibly have been created with the audience's needs in mind).

Your portfolio should cater for different opportunities and events. You don't need all of the following at any one time, but you won't know what you do need until the moment you need it. Luckily, the portfolio is something that can be built up with time. Even having just one thing (particularly if it is a telling story) is an excellent start.

Eventually your portfolio should contain:

a   At least three stories about specific problems that specific clients had that you specifically helped them solve.

   The stories should include explanations of what you did and why it worked (perhaps not too much detail: you want the listener to ask for more information). The stories should be structured as I recommend (in **63**) or better. Each story should have a short (ten second) version and a long one (up to a minute). 'At least three' really is a minimum: over time—years—there is, presumably, no reason why you shouldn't have dozens.

b   Some stories not about you or any of your clients, but ones that illustrate an important point about your services, or about you.

   These could be other businesses' stories (particularly if they're well known), they could be from the news, they could even be zen stories, whatever floats, as they say, your boat. You may take stories from my site, www.emotionalintelligenceatwork.com, and I will forgive you if, in the heat of conversation, you forget to attribute them to me—just don't pass them off as your own, because people don't like being deceived.

c   One or more pithy, and I mean pithy, statements of the services you provide.

   'I am an accountant and I work with small businesses and private individuals'. Full stop. 'I specialise in global corporate businesses.' Although this sort of thing shouldn't be the first thing you say, it would be discourteous not to answer a straight question promptly and well when asked it.

d   A pithy statement of the sort of person you are looking to meet.

This is not an exhaustive list but it could include several categories, only one of which (absolute maximum, two) you will say when asked this question on any particular occasion.

e   The answer to the question, 'What is the purpose of your business?'

This is not uppermost in business people's minds and I can't recall ever having been asked this question. Woe betide someone, however, who doesn't have a ready answer to the Smart Alec who asks you this. 'Mmm, I've not really thought about that before' will not impress the person cunning enough to ask in the first place.

As discussed earlier, it is a good way of describing what you do. You need to have a one sentence answer to this question. Ideally, you should have tested this out on a friend or colleague asking them to respond, each time you tell them a purpose, 'But that sounds rather like an outcome to me. If it were an outcome, what would the purpose of the business really be?'

f   The answer to the question, 'What outcomes does your business seek?'

If your business has lots of outcomes (and why not?) restrict yourself to two or three at any one time. Probably outcomes that relate to the success of your clients will be more appealing to the listener than ones relating to the length of the holidays you intend to take.

g   Some general material about what you do personally in the business.

As usual, this is best illustrated with a story. Of course, if you just answer the phone, it probably isn't worth replying, 'Well let me tell you a story. I was sitting in the office looking out of the window when suddenly the phone rang.

So I answered it. It was a wrong number.' And, if you reply, 'I am a communications facilitation expert, connecting callers to their selected staff member', don't be surprised to hear a groan from the other person.

h   Who you know.

Of course, what you reply in any one conversation will be determined by who you think the other person would like to meet. But, in general, if you have contacts in organisations who could be helpful, or you know connectors and mavens (described in **27**), it's worth saying more than just, 'I know Josephine Blogs'. Create a mini-spiel about what Josephine is willing to do for business people.

Your portfolio should *not* contain:

a   Rambling stories about anything.

b   Universal statements, such as 'I do anything for anyone'— even if it's true, it's not helpful.

c   Long spiels about the 'benefits' of your services or of what you do (see **46**). As above, a crisp statement of what you do is a courtesy, but the rest of the stuff most people go on about at networking events can be replaced by much more interesting material: the stories about how you helped the client solve their problem being at the heart of the matter.

d   Hesitations. You need to respond appropriately without pausing. This isn't difficult if you resolve (at least to start with) to answer any question, even one about the price of fish, with 'Let me answer that with a story…' and off you go with your favourite piscine story.

Remember:

○   people like stories

○   people learn and remember when they are in their feelings and a story puts them there

○   people can identify as much, or as little, as they choose with the actors in the story, so they feel comfortable.

Your portfolio should cover you for most eventualities; it's a generic thing. If you are preparing for a specific event, what you say at it is clearly specific to that event.

The portfolio should also include ad hoc items:

o knowledge of current and/or local news items, particularly those that are business-related

o opinions on current issues, for example the politics of the day (you may not be interested, but the other person may be)

o jokes (a much underrated form of content when networking).

54 Using your portfolio

If you are a trainer, coach, mentor, adviser, consultant perhaps, be prepared to have the unexpected opportunity to demonstrate your skills.

Story: Ad hoc presentation

Early on in my career as a business coach, I used to attend one client business's weekly briefings for staff. Otto, the boss, would spend around thirty minutes updating them with company news, discussing problematic clients, asking for their feedback on other clients and issues, giving them tips on how to subtly promote the business when they saw clients, telling them to clean their shoes and so on. Otto did a really good job and I found it fascinating watching him interacting with the rest of the staff, and watching them interact with him and each other.

On one occasion—I think it was the third or fourth day I was with them—Otto stood up at the beginning and announced 'I'm not doing the session today. Jeremy is.' And, with that, he sat down.

I had had no warning that he might do anything like that, and no notice. I had to start talking within fifteen seconds of him sitting down and run a thirty minute session for eight people, some of whom I didn't know very well. I don't think I consciously thought about it, I just used my intuition to pluck something from my portfolio and I made an interactive *session on the run in which each person had to assess their colleagues on various characteristics, such as positive/ negative, motivated away from/motivated towards and so on. It got very interesting when it turned out everyone in the business thought everyone else in the business, from Otto down, was reactive. No-one was proactive, and they were wondering why the business wasn't making progress.*

I had done this sort of exercise before and I knew that people tended to find it fun as well as interesting. The point is that I was confident enough to run a session on it without preparation. This type of session had been tucked into my portfolio some time earlier.

Story: Presentation

I used to attend one networking group's events assiduously. Each event had a speaker who gave a short presentation after the dessert. One day, the organiser came up to me after the meal had already started and asked me if would do the presentation for that event. I had little more than an hour, during which I was supposed to be hosting the particular table I was sitting at, to come up with something. Portfolio to the rescue once more.

The portfolio is especially valuable, nay, essential, in one-to-one meetings. I have lots of things I can show people in conversation—psychological models, business models, graphs and trends. They are either printed for use as I talk or (a speciality) I draw them from scratch on A4 sheets. Incidentally, people always ask for my sketches afterwards. Not, I think, because they are legible—they aren't—but because they remind the listener of what I said as I drew this line or wrote that word.

Firstly, identify what's going to be in your portfolio, collect it (or some of it), prepare and hone what you have and then practise it. Of course, this is something that will grow with time. Practise it on friendly business people you know, particularly in one-to-one meetings. These are ideal events to become fully proficient at explaining what you do. At one time, early in my business coaching career, I practised talking about my most complicated model thirty or forty times in a year, always to willing victims.

Practise it on family members or friends. If you don't have family or friends, practise on the dog. Or cat—'V. amusing. Love, Tiddles.'

55 What are you going to say about your business?

When you first start networking, you will need to do a lot of preparation each time so that you know what you are going to say.

In time, you will find that things you prepared for a specific event have a general use and so they will go into your portfolio. And other content will find its way there, too, thereby reducing what you need to do especially for a particular meeting. Eventually, you will be so practised that it will be all portfolio stuff supplemented by penetrating spur-of-the-moment insights and bon mots. At least, that's the idea.

a Definition and outline of the service you want to talk about at the networking event.

It's risky to talk about more than one thing to someone. They will get confused, you will run out of time, you might even get confused. Far, far better to stick to one service that you want to make the theme of your visit to an event. As I type this, I guess I will be going to a lot of events talking about this new book I have written. I will therefore resist regaling audiences with tales of my prowess as a business coach or trainer (unless they ask, of course).

The service you choose to talk about will obviously determine the stories and the problems you discuss.

b Stories about your business's clients.

If you are new to this game, then an absolute minimum of one, in a long and short version. The story should be directly relevant to the service you want to talk about.

You should have one or two in your portfolio, even at the beginning (I cannot emphasise too strongly that having enough material—and material you are confident of—is the best antidote to stage fright and nerves). As you get more experienced, you will have more clients to tell stories about *and* more stories to recall. In time, you should have dozens, literally.

c   The typical problems your clients bring you and how you help them solve them.

Not the same as stories. Stories are specific, probably true, accounts of real people. Talking about typical problems allows you to generalise; to focus on parts of the service you've decided to present at an event for which you do not yet have personal stories; to talk briefly about the market sector these problems occur in.

d   How does your business help clients solve these problems?

You are unlikely to get this far in a brief chat at a networking event. If you do, probably the best response is, 'Perhaps I could answer that by telling you about…' and off you go with a story.

e   What is the purpose of your business?

f   What outcomes does your business seek?

Both of these should be in your portfolio, and it is worth having them uppermost in your mind so that you stay focussed during conversations.

g   Who you would like to meet?

In my experience, people usually forget this, or don't realise how important it is. But, you don't know who the person you are talking to knows so, if you want to meet people in the construction sector, why not ask, 'Do you know anyone in the construction sector?' (A more nuanced question will probably serve you better; one that arises from a brief conversation with the other person to enable them to understand why you are asking.) As with the comments on stories, who you want to meet depends on what service you are proposing to talk about.

Story: Eggs (4)

Rex sat down at his desk, licked the end of his pencil and looked out of the window. He didn't have any stories about his business (at least not any that showed him in a good light) so he skipped that bit until he got to the next chapter. Having decided that his target market was the hospitality sector, he decided to research what hospitality sector networking opportunities there were. He found none. So he would have to go to more generic events and look for people who knew people in the hospitality sector.

This would require a different approach: people who know people in hospitality don't necessarily know anything about hospitality and, in particular, the pivotal position the egg plays in it.

So, he approached the headings above with a provisional attitude. He wouldn't really know what worked well until he had said it at a few events so it was pointless trying to make it perfect, or even good. It just had to be coherent.

a   Definition and outline of the service you want to talk about at the networking event.

Easy. Flogging eggs: high quality. Taste good. Ethically approved grass (or whatever chickens eat). Local supplier. He was confident he could riff on that easily (of course, he would have to refine his spiel soon if it was to have enough impact).

b   Stories about your business's clients.

Unfortunately no clients yet. This is actually a bonus, provided it doesn't go on too long. But he decided he would research similar businesses in other parts of the country and see what stories they had. Provided both businesses were comfortable from the point of view of competition, there was no doubt information he could give them in return.

c   The typical problems your clients bring you and how you help them to solve them.

Since talking about typical problems allows you to generalise, he imagined what these problems might be. The Torquay Towers hotel may have been slated by the Good Food Guide for the poor quality of its eggs at brekkers. The Eastbourne Towers hotel was receiving visitors' complaints about soldiers failing to stand up in yolk. And so on. If Rex had the chutzpah, he could actually tell obviously untrue but witty stories, if they had a kernel of truth in them.

d   How does your business help clients solve these problems?

Although, clearly, the primary way is through the quality of the ovoid foodstuffs, Rex was willing to provide a consultancy service, assisting clients to identify the right sort of eggs for their business.

e   What is the purpose of your business? and

f   What outcomes does your business seek?

Rex was certain he would have failed if the conversation ever got onto these points, in the early stages of networking. So he ignored them for now.

g   Who you would like to meet?

'I would like to meet people in the hospitality sector, particularly if they are involved in buying food or preparing menus.' This is clear, understandable, and sufficiently wide that it should generate some names soon.

To be continued…

56   What are you going to say about yourself?

For the sole trader, or micro-business, what you say about yourself may be quite close to what you say about your business. For the boss of a larger company, stories about what he or she does personally may be best illustrated by client stories. For a chairman, a non-executive director and so on, it is probably—but not invariably—more interesting for the listener to hear about their business than about them. Nevertheless, it's best to know what you are going to say when asked.

This is an opportunity to give a specific, and possibly long, answer and therefore should be avoided in a general networking event. But I have been to sit-down dinner events where there is clearly going to be a long time to chat to the two people either side of me. So, if the other person seems genuinely interested, why not go for it?

Your purpose in attending may not be the same as your business's purpose in having you attend. It seems to me that, when big banks show up at SME networking events, the bank's purpose is to explain to those attending how unspeakably wonderful the bank is, whereas the purpose of the individual in attending is to avoid being rapped on the knuckles for not being there.

It may be that, 'My purpose in attending is to develop my business in sector X, specifically doing service Y, and I am looking to pick people's brains about this sector'.

What do you want to get out of the event? That is, what are your outcomes? Worth having an answer in case the organiser asks you. Indeed, it may be worth telling the organiser whether they ask or not. Once you've said you want to find out more about sector X, so you can do Y, what you want to get out of the event must, at the very least, be some people to talk to about X and Y.

Who do you know? This is an important one for the other person. Yet, not knowing who they are in advance, it is hard to know whom they might want to know.

Sometimes, my chamber of commerce, Thames Valley, holds events for non-members to entice them into its clutches. Because I believe that, on balance, it's worth joining the chamber, I will explain to non-members at these events what they have to do, and who they ought to speak to, to maximise the value of membership. By naming names, I hope I can help get these novices to sign up, at the expense of giving the managers more work to do (and quite right, too).

57 How can you help other people?

You can help other people you meet at a networking event in a number of ways. You're unlikely to gain enough information from them to make a sensible offer of help in the hurly burly of the event itself, so your first priority is to get them on their own in a one-to-one follow-up meeting. Before that time, though, you can make a start at the networking event.

Clearly the objective is not to force your help onto everyone irrespective of their enthusiasm for the offer. You can only help those who either ask for it or appear to let you. Personally, if I find a novice networker at a chamber of commerce event who seems a little out of their depth, after a little conversation,

I say, 'May I make a suggestion?', and then—when given permission—I briefly outline the value of having a one-to-one with the organiser of the event. That's me being helpful.

It may become apparent that the other person needs a bookkeeper. If you know of one you could mention them (that's not an endorsement or a recommendation, but it's better than nothing). If you don't know a bookkeeper, you could offer to find one. This is where the true networker shines: they are willing to go, not the extra mile in this case, but the extra foot. It isn't hard to find the name of a bookkeeper at a networking event: you just ask the organiser. And you could suggest to the other person that that is what they should do. Better than nothing. But going and doing it for them is so much more stylish, and does your reputation good.

Ultimately, it's just about maintaining an attitude of helpfulness.

8 You need stories

58 People remember stories

Without a doubt, stories should form the most important parts of talking about what you and your business does. And, you will have noticed, this book is intentionally full of them. When pressed for time—and you should always be pressed for time—stories are the only thing worth talking about.

That may seem extraordinary, but the logic is clear. What is your purpose in being at a networking event? If it is to lecture others on your business, and what services it offers, so they can pass some hypothetical examination in the subject, good luck. But I can guarantee that everyone you give this information to will have forgotten it before they've even left the room.

If people at networking events tell me what they do, with the best will in the world I struggle to remember. If I do remember, I may well misunderstand it. The exchange is largely a waste of time for most people, given that most people aren't trained to ask questions or to listen to the answers. And they don't listen to answers because they are too busy thinking up their next question.

Further, nine times out of ten, after the first few words of the answer, the questioner loses interest because, let's face it, most people at networking events aren't really interested in what other people do: they're only really interested, *at that point*, in whether the other person might give them some work. (Don't mistake the veneer of British politeness for interest.)

So, I suggest that you should **set an intention to be remembered afterwards**. The intention is not the same thing as the *purpose* of networking. The purpose of networking is, as I've said, to find out how you can help others.

One should be remembered for being someone interesting—entertaining, even—someone worth talking to more. So, I suggest that, when asked 'What do you do?', you should reply, 'Let me answer that with a story'. This question is just a courtesy, but it does give the listener the opportunity to say 'No'. Never happened to me. Usually people signal they find a story a welcome, possibly even interesting, turn of events. And then you tell a story. As a representation of what you 'do', the story is likely to be incomplete, partial and possibly out of date. But, if told reasonably well, the story can be (*a*) interesting and (*b*) memorable.

Telling a story at a networking event marks out the teller as different from the crowd (in itself a good thing); and provides plenty of hooks for the other person to ask supplementary questions (particularly if the hooks have been deliberately placed there). The hooks generate enough of a conversation for one or both parties to determine whether they would like to have a follow-up meeting with the other, and this is the point of going to a networking meeting.

59 Mealtime

Sit down meals—where, politely, you are trapped between two people you don't know—offer their own challenges. But the principles are the same. These events often give you more time: you know it will be twenty minutes before the *crème brûlée* turns up—more *brûlée* than *crème*, usually—and, in my view, you have a duty to amuse other people at networking events, so get that portfolio out.

Story: *Chamber dinner*

I was sitting next to someone at a chamber dinner last week.
I had never met him before. He looked at my badge that said

'emotional intelligence at work' and asked me something like, 'What's that about?'

I said, mock-hesitatingly, 'Well, it's about, er, using emotional intelligence in the, er... at work'. He laughed, and he initiated a conversation about how he likes to use emotional intelligence in his workplace. Bingo. The conversation moved smoothly on to him. (Not me: I know he will find out what I do when he asks me, and I should wait until then. If he doesn't ask, he probably isn't that interested. This counsel is not perfect and I have encountered people who appear to have some sort of speech impediment preventing them from articulating the phrase, after they have been speaking solidly for half an hour about themselves and their business, 'So, what do you do then?')

And he opened up. He gave me all sorts of material directly relevant to what I do that led me to believe that he could, in fact, become a client. Meanwhile, because I carefully only said things that amplified and developed what he said (decorated with a few stories about past clients of mine), he was (I assume) getting the message that I knew what I was talking about. Thoughts were forming in his mind that I could be of use to his business (I know that because he said so).

The next morning, he got his LinkedIn contact request to me in pretty quickly (before I had even got up), with thanks for the conversation.

He did tell me early on that his firm was an accountants' practice. A piece of information I filed for later use.

60 Why stories are essential

Stories get people into their feelings.

Stories are essential to being remembered because:

a   Adults need to be in their feelings if they are to learn and remember.

b   People make decision in their feelings.

c   Telling a story makes you more entertaining and interesting—which is very good even if it has no other benefits.

d   Telling a story makes you different from most of the people in the room, all of whom are trying to tell everyone else what they do—which is also good in itself.

Telling stories is one way of being entertaining. And I try to make my stories amusing, too. Laughing is an emotional response, not an intellectual one. Getting the other person to laugh—or smile—is really important. People—particularly women, who are often less at ease in networking events than are men—really like people who are funny. And I practise telling my stories. I practise making the pauses and the asides seem natural, and I practise making the jokes seem spontaneous. One of my stories starts, 'I had a client. He was an ex-policeman. Actually, I suppose he still is an ex-policeman.' (It is, of course, how you tell it that matters.) And that still gets a laugh, years after I first thought of it.

Adults learn best when they are in their feelings. As you don't have a lot of time at a networking event, you need to exploit this. People usually get into their feelings as a result of an experience and, in the circumstances, telling them a story is a good way of giving them an experience. Of course, going and showing them, introducing them to the client and so forth, would be much better, but you don't have the opportunity to do that at a networking event (though you could do later, if you tell them a good enough story).

Stories are good because they are not about the person you are talking to. That person can choose the extent to which they identify with the subject of the story. If you are lucky, you may be describing a problem that the person has (or that a person they know has), but you don't know that, and they know you don't know. Having revealed that your client solved their problem thanks to you, you obviously are in a far stronger position—because the person you are talking to will get that, even though they don't mention it.

Even if the problem is unfamiliar to the person you are talking to, they can still empathise with the subject of your story. And **empathy** is the feeling you want them to have. This is why you need to labour the problems the client had in order to get a big contrast between what life was like for the client before they met you and what it was like afterwards. When people empathise with the subject of the story, they're in their feelings and they are much more likely to remember you and have at least a vague remembrance of how you helped others.

Stories allow the listener to identify with the subject of the story as little or as much as they want to.

61 Cut your cloth to fit your coat

For each story that you plan to tell at networking events (if you get the chance), you need different versions: short and long. You need to assess how long you have in which to tell the story before you start, because a story cut short, if you're telling it well, is a real disappointment to the listener and you can't recapture their attention later.

Here's an example of cutting the story to fit the time available:

o (Version 1) 'May I answer that with a story? I was working with a client recently whose problem was X. Well, that's what they thought, but actually we worked out it was Y. This proved a bit tricky to address, because of P, Q and R. In the end they decided to do A, B and C. And, as a result, E and F happened for the client.'

Note, there is nothing about the person talking (the 'I' of the story). It's all about the client, what their problem was (and wasn't) and what they did to sort it out. Talking about clients helps the listener identify with the subject of the story and prompts them to think of people they know who might be in a similar position (including themselves, obviously).

At a deeper level, not only do people like stories but, as we have seen, stories get them into their feelings. They need to be in their feelings if you want them to learn something (that is, get an idea of what you do), if you want them to make a decision (that is, to have that follow-up meeting) or if you simply want them to remember you.

A shorter version of this story goes:

o (Version 2) 'May I answer that with a story? I was working with a client recently whose problem was X. Well, that's what they thought, but actually we worked out it was Y. This proved a bit tricky to address, because of P, Q and R. So, as a result, E and F happened for the client.'

Even shorter:

o (Version 3) 'May I answer that with a story? I was working with a client recently whose problem was X. Well, that's what they thought, but actually we worked out it was Y. In the end, E happened for the client.'

Note that, however short, I won't let go of, 'but actually we worked out it was Y'. This is crucial because it sets the teller apart from all the other businesses who could have provided the same service. A marketing person shouldn't be promoting their ability to do marketing; they should be promoting their ability to find out the best marketing to do for each particular client.

I use the word 'we' in these little stories because I am assuming the teller doesn't want the listener to get the impression that he/she simply instructs the client what to do. If the teller does instruct clients what to do, they should say so. On the whole, it is best if service providers at least give the impression that they involve the client in decisions about their business.

Of course, the person must really have engaged their prospect/client in a discussion of whether X was in fact the problem.

If you don't have a story about a particular type of problem, you can say:

o 'May I answer that with a story? A colleague of mine was working with a client recently whose problem was X.'

…provided you know someone for whom this is true.

If you've just started your business and you have no clients and no colleagues, it is legitimate to say:

o 'I was reading an article/watching a video/talking to someone at a networking event/etc about a business whose problem was X and what happened was…'

As a last resort, make something up—but tell your listener that you have done so. To the question, 'What do you do?', say something like:

o 'The sort of business I want to work with might have problem X. Let's call it Henry Bloggins Ltd. In that case, I would…'

Giving the fictitious business a name gives the listener something to latch on to. Of course commercial confidentiality prevents you from doing that when telling true stories (unless you know the client is happy to named—and some are, particularly if the story reflects well on them).

62 Refining your stories

Stories are memorable in ways that dry factual statements aren't, particularly when people are listening to a number of other people for the first time all telling them what they do. Any idea that the story is not as accurate as the factual information (even if that is true) is irrelevant if the choice is between being remembered and not being remembered.

The point is that your purpose is not to give facts (they can come later, if they are needed): it's to give people an impression of you and your business that the other person can remember. Of course, if you suggest that Lord Sugar is in the habit of sending you cases of champagne, such is the value he places on your advice, it had better be true. But, if it were true, I don't think it is the first thing you should say, because it doesn't shed any light on how your advice assists the noble Lord.

Here are some tips to productive story telling as part of your promotional activities:

a   Develop as many stories as you can, illustrating different facets of the services you offer. Develop a short (ten seconds) version and a long one (up to a minute) of each.

b   Make the story about the problem the client had and what you did to help them resolve it. Explanations of why your intervention worked are unlikely to be important if only because, if you tell the story well, the other person is bound to ask you. (It's always better to have the other person approach you for information rather than have to push yourself on them all the time. Queen Victoria was forever complaining that Gladstone addressed her as though she were 'a public meeting'.)

c   Add specific detail—it was a car manufacturer, it was a hotel, whatever. The detail may be irrelevant to the point of the story, but it is not irrelevant to why you're telling the story: detail better locates the story in reality and that makes it more likely to be remembered.

d   Be careful naming names: people may not like what they thought was confidential being talked about in public, particularly if it is not that favourable to them. I have never had a problem with using aliases and even drawing attention to the fact ('I had a client, let's call her Susan. Susan was this…Susan did that…'). By doing so, it might reassure a possible client that their secrets are safe with you, too.

e   Strip out the details that are about you (not the client): for example, don't say things like 'It was a long time ago' or 'I don't really work in that area any more' (which I have actually heard), don't say why or how you got to meet the client, unless it is directly relevant to your point.

f   Labour the point about the difficulties the client was having before they met you.

g   Be careful about how you stop. The ending is what the other person is likely to remember most. If you want to pique their interest, you have to leave something unsaid in order to prompt a question like, 'Well how did you do that, then?' On the other hand, finish too early and they will feel irritated at being left high and dry. Avoid postscripts. If the other person thinks you've stopped, they won't be listening (or they will resent having to listen some more). If you restart, say, 'As a postscript, what happened was X'. But, if X is relevant, it should have been woven into the main story.

h   Morals. Many stories have a moral: the lesson you want the other person to learn. Whether you include one has to be a matter of judgement for each story and for each situation. They can come across as statements of the bleedin' obvious, or they can fall into the postscript trap. But they can also be a very neat way of repeating the essence of the story in a few words. If you say, 'And the moral is…', it's clear that the story is over but you haven't quite stopped talking.

i   Practise your stories at every opportunity. They will not be right first time, so be curious as to what goes down well with people and the reasons why they lose interest.

j   Continuously refine your stories. Is one of them too short? (Unlikely.) Is it too long? (Probably.) Have you missed something important? Have you used jargon? (If so, remove it: explaining it just clogs up the story, and not explaining it is discourteous.)

Incidentally, it doesn't matter if the story is incomplete. In fact, I would urge you to cultivate incomplete statements, explanations and presentations at networking events. It is in the one-to-ones later that we create our network, and leaving a few questions unanswered in the listener's mind at a networking event will encourage them to welcome the invitation to a one-to-one to find out the answers.

63   Structure your stories well

There are many structures that story tellers can use. But some structures are more useful than others for the purpose of networking. Before considering one that works, it is worth remembering the following:

a   The point of the story is to show the listener that the teller has the ability to help clients solve their problems. It isn't to educate the listener, so it doesn't have to be complete. The listener isn't going to have to sit an exam afterwards on it. And, of course, it has to be memorable.

b   All detail that is extraneous to this objective should be eliminated—however interesting and however much the teller thinks it should be included.

c   Because the point of telling the story is to show the listener that the teller has the ability to help clients solve their problems, the emphasis should be on the skills, abilities and attributes the teller brought to the situation, not primarily what the teller did—however interesting.

d   Important. When preparing the story, imagine that the listener interrupts you saying 'But what did you *really* bring to the situation?', 'Why did the client have to employ *you*, rather than anybody else?'. In my experience, most people miss this crucial bit out.

e   Most people would benefit from thinking harder about how their unique background and professional experiences are helpful to others. It's got nothing to do with 'Unique selling proposition' and everything to do with your specialisms, your specific experience, your ability to be insightful, what makes you gel with clients and all the rest of it.

The structure is in five parts, as follows.

a   Introduction

This is optional and sets the scene where necessary: it should be as brief as possible. It is intended to ensure the listener has some context for the story. It is best if it doesn't contain specific information on which an understanding of the story relies. This is because you are getting ahead of yourself: this information belongs in the next part.

b   Exposition

This is where you describe the problem the client had before you arrived. You need to describe it as clearly (but concisely) as possible, and make sure the description can be matched later when you explain how you helped the client solve it.

It is essential that this is not a dry, neutral, factual description. You need to 'milk' it. Really get across the emotions the client must have been feeling, the difficulty his/her business was having and the complexity (no doubt) that was going to greet you when you arrived.

The problem wasn't, for example, that the client had an inefficient accounts system. The problem was that staff were moaning about staying late, invoices were sent late, the boss was stressed, his/her spouse was giving the boss a hard time that made them more stressed and so on.

You need to create an emotional 'drop' between the start and end of the exposition because, if you are going to get the listener into their feelings, this drop is a good way of doing it.

If someone is in their feelings, they are primed to learn. In this case, all that is needed is that they remember the experience of the drop long enough that, in their feelings, they are most likely to remember what you say next. Which is…

c   Crisis

This term is taken from ancient Greek drama, where it means 'turning point'. It *could* coincide with your arrival into the story, though that probably happened during the exposition, where you recount the problems that you discovered.

Ideally, the turning point should be a revelation, a realisation that the client had as a result of your involvement. Now they know why they have had those problems. They are confident that you understand the problem, know how it can be fixed and help them do that.

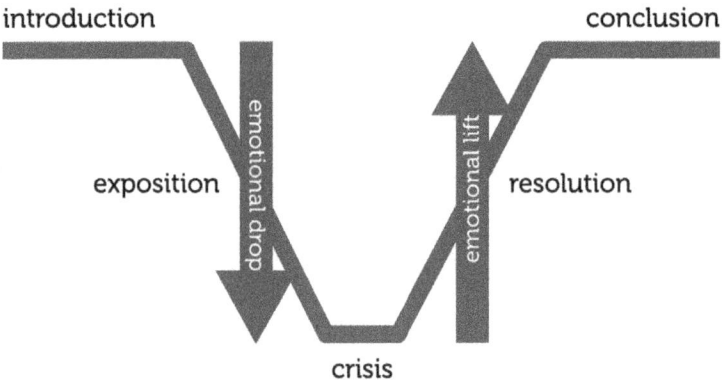

d   *Resolution*

In this part you describe how your involvement enabled the client to resolve their problem. It should have an air of things getting better, people feeling more positive. Once again, it is essential that this is not a dry, neutral, factual description. Again, you need to 'milk' it. And, as much as possible, emphasise what *you* really brought to the client as opposed to the tasks you actually carried out—unless those tasks were so exceptional that they are the point of the story.

What 'you really brought to the client' is a must-have really. If you have exceptional capacity to make links and draw connections, say so. If you are unusually good at seeing underlying causes, say so. Most other people don't have these precise skills and, if they do, it doesn't occur to them to say so. Yet one of them might have been the single most important ability of yours that enabled the problem to be solved. It may be that the boss has drawn around themselves people who are like them: all 'detail people'. Your capacity to see the broader picture was invaluable to them.

Everyone has a particular (even if not unique) ability, or mix of abilities, that they should be talking about. If you don't believe you have any, hire a coach to help you dig them out. Seriously.

You need to create an emotional 'lift' between the start and end of the resolution part to enable the listener to enjoy an emotional release from the bad feelings they were in, I hope, just before the crisis. (You definitely don't want to leave them on a low!) As that release will accompany your explanation of your involvement in the problem, the two will become associated.

e   Conclusion

You do not want the listener to end up on an emotional high either (because the moment you leave, that emotional level will sag). They should be just above the neutral state they were in before you started. So the conclusion just allows them to land gently. However, it should be brief and could be omitted, if appropriate.

64 Write your own stories

It's often worth thinking up an obviously fictional story that underlines a point you want to make about the services you offer. Here's one of mine. It's clearly not true, and I modify it heavily depending on my audience and the time I have available. In fact, this version is explicitly the print version: I've never actually told it, word for word, as it stands here.

(This story was prompted by a genuine piece of 'research' commissioned by a manufacturer of power drills. The 'research' discovered that people don't buy drills for the sake of owning a drill; they buy the hole in the wall that the drill makes.)

Story: Drill

Apart from a few odd individuals, people don't buy power tools so they can slip into the garage and caress them. They buy an electric drill because they need a hole in the wall.

In other words, when you need to establish what a business needs—whether they are a prospect or a client—it's as well not to take the first thing they say at face value.

a   So, if Matt says he needs an electric drill, he's really saying he needs a hole in the wall.

b   However, perhaps there is a cheaper, quicker or more effective way of making that hole (like a pointed stick, perhaps).

c   Does someone really need a hole in the wall? Perhaps Matt is making an avant-garde art installation. Probably not. More likely, Matt needs to be able to make holes in the wall because he needs to put up a bookshelf. That's much more plausible.

d   But is that the end of the story? After all, a bookshelf in itself is not usually a lovely object to have on the wall. No, Matt needs a bookshelf to house the books that are currently piled up on the floor.

e   Is that the end of the story? No. As it happens, Matt is tired of being nagged—sorry, reminded—by his partner that he said some time ago he would do something about those books, and what he really needs is for the reminding to stop.

f   As it happens, things haven't been going well between Matt and his partner and the row about the books is just one example of, unfortunately, many. Probably what Matt really needs is some relationship counselling.

So, as I said, it pays not to take things at face value.

Of course, the books do have to be housed and a bookshelf is probably a good way of doing this. It is a problem—but not the problem.

I make that six layers under the presenting one of 'I need a drill'. If you can get to the bottom of what a business person really needs, as opposed to (a) what they think they need, and/or (b) what they would like you to think they need, and then can recommend a suitable supplier, then you will have a business friend for life.

Almost all of the stories in this book are true, but disguised. I made up the chain of stories *Eggs* because I don't have a case study that suits my purposes in this book.

Story: Eggs (5)

Rex didn't have any clients so, if he was going to tell stories, they had to be made up or come from other people. He decided that, under the circumstances, there's not a lot you can make up about an egg, so he decided to do some more research. He would contact people in the hospitality industry and ask what their problems were regarding food buying and finding suppliers of products to their desired level of quality. He was banking on the fact that, provided he was careful not to give the slightest hint that he was selling, people, unless we are very busy, love talking about ourselves.

In fact, Rex got quite a few rebuffs. But he got three or four stories—none of them about eggs, but no matter—that he felt could be useful. One or two of them were founded in the contact's deep belief that the quality of foodstuffs was paramount. He noted them for future engagement.

One of Rex's problems was that he couldn't talk about the reliability of his business (because it was too young) and talking about another business's reliability was irrelevant. He decided to cross that selling point off his list until he could substantiate it and hope it didn't come up too often.

To be continued…

65 Use other people's stories

…provided they are out of copyright; or retell them in your own words. (There is no copyright on ideas in either the UK or the USA.)

This story, in various versions, is well known. I use it to help people understand my role in the client's business (that is, I am not hands-on, working *in* the business, I am definitely working, with them, *on* the business). And to free up people's expectations about what they are paying for when they buy my services.

Story: Submarine

The navy's most advanced submarine came to a halt and eventually limped into port. The best repairers in the country were contacted but none was able to fix the boat. In desperation, the navy called one notoriously difficult man.

He duly arrived, walked around the boat and eventually came to a halt in front of a pipe. Taking out a small hammer, he hit it gently. Amazingly, the submarine shuddered back to life.

The navy was very grateful and asked the man to send his invoice. However, when it arrived, they were disconcerted to find it was for £100,000. Summoning the man, they complained that this was far too much for simply hitting a pipe with a hammer. Would he please resubmit his invoice in more detail?

So the man resubmitted:

'For hitting the submarine with a hammer, £100.
For knowing where to hit the submarine with a hammer, £99,900.'

And here is a story within a story: one is a true one about a client, the other is a 'zen story' (a very useful type of story worth investigating).

Story: Monks and the lady of the night

Two travelling monks reached a ford in a river where they met a young lady of the night. Wary of the current, she asked if they would carry her across. One of the monks hesitated, but the other quickly picked her up onto his shoulders. Together the monks strode through the river until they reached the other side. The monk set the woman down on the other bank. She thanked him and continued her journey.

But the happy conversation they had experienced up until the river had stopped. As the monks continued on their way, one was brooding and preoccupied. Eventually, unable to hold his silence, he spoke with anger. 'Brother, our spiritual training teaches us to avoid any contact with women—let alone that sort of woman—but you picked that one up on your shoulders and carried her!'

'Brother,' the second monk replied, 'I set her down on the other side, while you are still carrying her.'

Now, Brian and Jeff's business is still in its early years. Although showing every sign of success, like all businesses in startup it has been vulnerable to untoward events.

Last year, a staff member behaved completely out of character—and in a highly damaging way that seriously threatened the business. The staff member left, eventually the situation was sorted out, and the business has now returned to its profitable course.

Inevitably, Brian and Jeff were very hurt by this person's behaviour and found it hard to get over their anger and their feelings of being let down. Jeff, in particular, nursed his sense of betrayal and anger for months. Outwardly calm and professional, inwardly he was seething.

Some months after these events, I was talking to Jeff and Brian. Among other things in our conversation, I told them the story of the monks and the lady of the night.

And then, a few more months on, I bumped into Jeff. We fell to talking about his business, which was really moving forward now. I asked how he was and he replied that, of all the things I had previously said to him, that story had been the most powerful. It had really enabled him to see that he was carrying his anger long after it was appropriate. He was then able to ask himself whether it was helpful to carry on doing so and he decided to let go of it.

When people nurse these sorts of feelings—grudges, slights, hurts, anger, resentment, bad temper, even illness—they are usually directed at one or other person. Yet, for that person, the precipitating event is long in the past, they have moved on and, in particular, they are not interested in the other person's feelings on the subject.

The angry person is probably nursing a sense of righteousness (and they probably were right), a belief in the justification of their grievance (and it probably was justified) and a sense in which their anger is an attack on the other person—and boy do they deserve it!

But the other person isn't there anymore. And that was then and this is now.

What Jeff learnt was that it wasn't the employee who was 'making him angry' by their actions. He was making himself angry—and perpetuating it. The only person doing the hurting was himself. But, if he wanted it to stop, all he had to do was choose to drop the anger and discover that it had gone.

Even if (and I don't believe this) nursing anger is a legitimate activity in one's personal life, under what circumstances can it possibly be a valid business tactic for the co-owner of a business?

66 Particular stories for particular situations and people

There's a danger that, in writing enthusiastically about telling stories, I give the impression that it's difficult. It isn't. My purpose is to help you do it well in a restricted time period. So, in this topic, I want to suggest that you should have dozens of stories. Unless you have really only just started out in business, it's probably quite likely that you can recall dozens of incidents in your work life that are potentially illuminating.

Why would you need so many? Simply, because you want to have the maximum choice in any particular situation. For example, if you are networking with people who predominantly work in or supply to the health sector, a few health-related stories could come in handy. On the other hand, and particularly if you are in the health sector or supply it, a few stories explicitly not about the health sector could be better (on the principle that people learn when the possibility of preconceived ideas is minimised). Indeed, one of my refrains when talking to both the public sector and the third (that is, charitable) sector is the value of them considering being more businesslike: adopting the good from commercial practice while steering clear of the bad.

These stories need to be in your portfolio. It may be that some fall by the wayside. You will find out for yourself which stories chime with people and which are less effective. Don't discard any of them, but promote the best to your portfolio.

67 The 'perfect' short presentation

Some networking groups require people to talk for one or two minutes to some or all of the group. I'm assuming that a small presentation at a networking event will be about your business, though there is no reason in principle why it shouldn't be about pigeon fancying, particularly if you can shoe-horn a plausible business point into the presentation. It will certainly get you remembered. As usual, if your purpose is to sell to the audience, it will immediately be detected and resented.

Story: IFA

Gareth was a financial adviser, a difficult service to describe and maintain interest in even over a short time. So he spent almost all of his two minutes telling a story. This story was about one of his clients who owned and ran a small business, employing a small number of staff. As is often the case his wife had a job in the firm. He and his wife realised there were no processes in place should the unimaginable happen, and he fell under a bus. She could not even access the company's bank account. So Gareth spent some time with the man and his wife defining all the processes that needed to be put in place and then went on to set them all up.

A couple of months later, the man had a stroke and was effectively removed from the business for, as it seemed at the time, perpetuity. All the processes Gareth had set up did their job. His wife took over the helm temporarily and the company was able to carry on.

Happily, the client was able to go back to work after many months' recuperation.

Gareth was an excellent story teller and he had clearly learnt his story. He told it in a far more compelling way than I have here. In truth, of the many thousands of two minute presentations I have heard, his has been the single best two minute presentation so far.

In any presentation of two minutes or less, I suggest you should allocate:

○ three quarters to a good story

○ one quarter to wrap up the story, thus:

- I do X (for example, 'I am a financial adviser')
- and my company is Y (if you must, 'We offer a number of services including A, B and C')
- The sort of person I am looking to meet is...
- 'I would be delighted to have a one-to-one with each of you', and hand out your business card.

So, my suggestion that you need a 'long' version of stories fits here. You will finish within the time available and everyone will be grateful. They may even take your example as something from which they can learn.

9 What you should be doing at the networking event

68 Don't forget the leadership precept: make it about the other person

As we have seen, if you have never been networking before, and if you have never spoken to anyone about your business before, the temptation is to talk about the services you offer and their benefits. This is human nature. It isn't wrong. It is just that, counterintuitively, it isn't the most useful thing to do. And it could be harmful.

So, a business person who has never been networking before, and has never spoken to anyone about their business before, will need some convincing that talking to other people about *their* business, possibly even promoting those people's businesses, is a more efficient use of their time. In other words, it's all about other people.

However, for those for whom this is a novelty—a scary novelty—I suggest try it. Try it for one networking event. Put the needs of the people you meet ahead of your needs. At the end of the meeting, you will have a short to-do list. Then do those things. It may take an hour or two.

This works better still if you commit to doing it for a few meetings—for a month, say. If you are seen to help others, some people will in time help you. If you do it repeatedly you will get a reputation for being a 'good guy/gal' and people will warm to you even if you've never spoken to them.

The trouble is that there is no neutral position. If you decide that 'I shall neither help nor hinder others', you will fade away. Your attractiveness will drop because, frankly, a non-position is not an attractive one to take.

69 Be entertaining

Think of it as a show. Or at least act as if it were. This topic is an excuse to remind you that:

a   Your portfolio needs to be full of *interesting* things—facts from current affairs, things you have learnt in web articles—things that will pique the other person's interest.

b   You need brief, succinct information about your business and a few of your clients.

c   You need a variety of stories about yourself and your business—preferably relevant and certainly interesting—of varying lengths.

I am tempted to learn some magic tricks in case the conversation at networking events starts to flag.

You should ask questions about what the other person is saying to you. 'Why?' is good enough, but many people find that a little too direct. 'How come?' is better. You can often get away with a '… because…?' if someone seems reluctant to go into a lot of detail (if only out of consideration for you and your presumed boredom threshold). On the whole, interjections such as, 'Jesus! You did *what?!*' are to be avoided as others find them off-putting.

Once you have something from the other person, and bearing in mind it is supposed to be a conversation after all, see what you can reply that is relevant. This shouldn't be about you. An accountant might be explaining how they can reduce their clients' tax liability, so you remark something like, 'Oh yes, like Joe Smith who I see in the news has only paid four pence in tax this year'. (Joe Smith is not a real person. At least, this Joe Smith isn't.) The other person will love the chance to share their professional, insider knowledge and explain in detail how Smith got away with it.

Being provocative is fine, *provided*—and this is important—your remarks cannot conceivably be construed as a criticism of, or attack on, the other person. (And, preferably, not as an attack on anyone.) Bear in mind that the more events you go to and the more people you talk to at each one, you will be increasingly confident who you can tease or provoke and who you should keep a straight face with.

For example, if some people ask me, 'What do you do?', I might say, 'To be honest, I'm not really sure. I just talk to people. They seem to find it useful, so I invoice them and they pay me.' Other people deserve a more serious response.

70 Be different

On principle. Being different is a good precept for business generally. It offers a variety of choice to the customer and, for business people hung up about USPs, it offers a partial solution (the other part being to get over it).

Simply by applying the ideas in this book, you'll be significantly different from other people at networking events as well as, I trust, being successful at networking. Otherwise, be aware of how other people are behaving at networking events; what they are saying, whether the conversation is one-sided or not. It's worth being a people watcher.

Stop trying to prove you are an expert. This is one of the most annoying habits that people display at networking events (second only to selling, in fact). And, it's much worse online. Most people you meet in networking events are unlikely to be experts in their field; we are all learning. And the funny thing is that people who really are experts rarely feel the need to bang on about it all the time.

More to the point, a networking event is not a place to demonstrate your prowess: the follow-up one-to-one is the place for that, if it is necessary at all. If there is any message worth getting across in a networking event, it is that you have a clue what the other person is talking about and, if you can't deal with their problem, you know someone who can.

What you can do is tell people interesting stuff. For example, it is actually possible to make search engine optimisation interesting—as I found out only today.

71 Find and cultivate the connectors, mavens and influencers

Connectors, mavens and influencers are covered in **27**. These benign roles can form the basis of very useful relationships. They recognise that some people actually like networking so much they develop it into, not necessarily an art form, but at least an organised, thought-through way of helping others. This means not only that they can help you, but they are actually willing and keen to do so.

The people who run networking events—particularly if you have paid for admission and, even more particularly, if you have had to pay a membership fee to join the 'club'—are people whom you should work ruthlessly in your networking interests. They really should be connectors and mavens. There is no excuse for them not volunteering:

o   the names of people in their organisation, or outside it for that matter, who could be of interest to you

o   to introduce you to these people.

If they don't volunteer, you might have to ask them to volunteer. Of course, you will have to have briefed them well, for which a sit-down one-to-one meeting is necessary. If they have no understanding of what you do and no idea of who you'd like to meet, it will hardly be surprising that they don't help you. And herein lies an interesting observation. If every member of a chamber of commerce or networking organisation demanded these services of the management, it would be swamped. So this advice relies, I am afraid, on most of the members not making use of this very valuable resource.

Most such people are only too pleased to help. They are likely to go the extra mile if you are willing to offer a *quid quo pro*—for example, to do a presentation at a networking lunch when their scheduled speaker drops out. You will soon be the scheduled speaker.

So, while you should feel entitled to have these services as part of your membership fee, it's best not to demand them but to ask for them. Create a context in which they know, like and trust you and want to help.

72 Don't, under any circumstances, sell anything to anyone

We've been through this already. At one level, my injunction, 'Don't sell' is mere pedantic attention to the meaning of words. However, this statement has many layers and, at bottom, it is the fundamental reason why some people are good at getting clients and others aren't or can't; why some people shift large quantities of widgets, and others move none. The 'standard model' is that you've got to 'sell' to them.

My problem with this is that 'selling' is about making the vendor's need to have someone become a client more important than the client's need to find the right solutions to their business issues. Trying to sell in a networking meeting is crass. You have little or no information about what the other person really needs, or whether they have the slightest interest in buying anything from anyone.

My advice goes so far as to not give out business cards unless asked for one. Wait to be asked for your card. If you can't bear to wait, at least ask if you may give them your card. No-one will say no, though they might bin it when they get back to the office. (Because if they had really wanted it, they really would have asked you for it.)

The point of all this is that you cannot make people buy your stuff (or, if you manage to do this, be prepared for a string of complaints and disappointment). Some people sell because they are running a scarcity model that impels them to behave like this. I'm not against running a scarcity model. All I am saying is that, creating a situation in which the prospective client asks to come on board is as easy as ramming your services down their throat and likely to generate far more good will, commitment and further business.

I hope I dissuaded you from *elevator pitches* in **20**. They really are the epitome of self-centred selling, having no respect for the interests or sensibilities of the victim. They are seemingly designed to inflict the greatest possible damage to the vendor's reputation while minimising the chance that the vendor will ever get to talk to the victim in happier circumstances.

Still, business people attempt to do it. Still, networking organisations promote their events by saying there will be a speaker telling you how to improve your elevator pitches. It really is so depressing.

If you were in the happy position of getting into a lift only to discover a potential benefactor or big prospect already there, make your objective be to get a second meeting, in their office. So, how will you get that second meeting by what you say in the lift? (Because a rushed, garbled, incomplete elevator pitch certainly won't do it.)

You pique their interest. You say something brief that is designed to have them reply, 'That's interesting, tell me more'.

You need to be specific. That means you have to be able to adapt a portfolio story instantly to what you perceive to be the interests of Sir Alan or Sir Richard or… (this is why the elevator pitch is such a silly idea).

Personally, I like quotations and can remember quite a few of them. For me, my ideal lift companion will be interested in leadership and change. So, I have memorised some quotations about these subjects and would pull one out if the need ever arose.

73   Ask for help

There are people who would rather die than ask for help (mostly men). They may be in a small minority (and may not be around for long), but the proportion of people who wait until the situation is desperate is substantial. Of course, this is true of life in general but, in a networking context, where one is surrounded by people all claiming that their businesses are surging forward, it is easy to assume that we are the only person struggling.

I take the rather harsh view that, if an individual in their private life wishes not to ask for help, that's fine. But, when a business person is representing their business, it is the business that suffers if the individual decides to adopt this attitude. If the business has staff, there is a wholly unnecessary risk to their jobs, or at least to their next pay rise.

And the funny thing is that, by and large, other people do want to help. By and large those who want to help do so without judging or gloating. The story of the person who needs help is too close to the bone for most of them.

So, if you need help, just ask. You may need to think about who you are going to ask, and maybe the event organiser is the starting point. The issues that people have that prevent them from asking for help are often based in embarrassment, sometimes guilt and even shame, and these are topics outside the remit of this book. However, if you do feel guilty or even ashamed, it will be worth thinking about where this has come from. If you can work that out, I bet it has nothing whatsoever to do with you as an adult or with your business. As one client, then aged forty, said to me, 'Do you realise I've been doing that [damaging behaviour] since I was a little boy?'

There is a vast wealth of expertise in any group of people at a networking event so why not tap into it? Wordpress may be driving you up the wall, or you want some free legal advice, or you are even having trouble 'converting' sales leads into clients: there's bound to be someone there only too willing to show off their skills by helping you. And, if they do help, why not help them by mentioning them to others needing the same services?

I got my graphic designer by asking the host of a networking event whom he would recommend. Although the designer and I went through the formalities of a one-to-one meeting and he showed me his portfolio (which was interesting), actually I had made my mind up on the basis of the recommendation and, of course, his own website that showed me what his work was like.

74 Talk to a range of people

At one level, this is too obvious to be worth saying, but we really should move around the room.

It's just too easy to hang onto one person because it is hard work going up to the next one; and the other person is only too pleased they have you to talk to because then they don't have to find someone else to talk to either.

After five minutes, say:

o 'I must circulate/talk to that person over there.'

o 'It was good to talk, let's have a one-to-one meeting.'

o 'Who in the room do you think I should be talking to?'

Interrupt other people. A networking event is not the place for two people to hold a private conversation. Of course, if we can interrupt light-heartedly, it helps a lot:

o 'I'm new here. Who are you?'

o 'I'm not new here, but we haven't met, is this your first time?'

o 'Good to see you again.'

o 'Do you think that waiter is a witch?'

…and all these other really easy starters are 'allowed'. In any case, maybe they're both desperate to be interrupted, such is the depth of languor to which their conversation has sunk.

In any case a very simple, 'May I interrupt you?' is perfectly acceptable and dares the other people to say 'No'. That said, in all cases, wait until an opportune moment: be polite, it goes without saying. Wait until one person has finished their story of how they cremated their pet rabbit using a do-it-yourself kit they bought off the internet.

Talk to people we may not believe can help us but whom we might be able to help. 'Nuff said. You know why I say this.

10 Getting the most from a conversation

75 If you are tongue-tied

Some people allow themselves to let the moment just before they open their mouth be the most stressful.

Opening gambits need only start the ball rolling. It doesn't matter if they are innocuous provided the conversation doesn't stay innocuous:

- 'What do you do?' is perfectly acceptable; this is a business networking event after all. Or, 'What does your business do?' You may even get a story back.

- 'Do you find these events useful?', assuming that the event is one of a series.

- 'How are you finding this event?'/'Is this event proving useful?'

- If it's after the speaker/meal: 'What did you think of the speaker/meal?' 'Did you agree with the speaker when she said…?' Or, 'Did the salmon pâté agree with you?'

- In desperation, you might look around you: 'God, this carpet's awful!'

Even 'Hello, how are you?' works.

Then again, play the newbie card, if it is true:

o   'I'm new here, who do think I should talk to?'
o   'Who are the leading lights?'
o   'Why are you here?'
o   'What do you get from this event?'
o   'Are you a member of the chamber/club?'
o   'Do you come here often?'

In truth, almost anything will do, providing you relieve the other person of their difficulty in trying to think of an opening gambit.

You should play the connector and maven cards: basically ask who the connectors and mavens in the room are and see if you can get an introduction to one or two of them.

One class of person to approach is the person standing by themselves (the wallflower). This person is almost certainly new to networking, or at least new to that event, and may be at a loss. My chamber of commerce gives attenders lists of the other attenders (or at least those who have booked). This gives the newbie the excuse of earnestly perusing the list to decide who he is going to talk to rather than actually talking to anybody. (And it is a he: women are much better at supporting each other in this sort of situation.) Rescue them.

If you're asked, 'What do you do?', don't tell them. Tell them a story (see section 8). Use the resources in your portfolio. It's hard to do this without mentioning at some point what you do. That's not a problem. Most people work it out ('…and when I finished designing the tallest building on the planet…'; 'Oh, so you're an expert in email marketing, then?').

76 Keeping the conversation going

As the conversation continues, resist the temptation to say anything along the lines of 'that happened to me'. That is an attempt to regain control of the conversation disguised as sympathy. Keep it about them. Prompt them with follow-up questions. If your opening gambit was 'What do you do?', and you get a response of some kind, try:

o 'What do you enjoy about that?'

o 'What do you least enjoy about that?'

o 'What sort of clients do you have?'

o 'Who would you like as a client?', if you want to get to the point quickly.

o 'Why do they go to you?'

o Occasionally, I try, 'Do tell me a story about one of your clients'. This isn't usually welcomed because the other person hasn't thought about stories. You risk getting a rambling unstructured monologue, as they play willing, from which, out of sheer humanity, you have to extricate them sooner or later.

o A simple 'Tell me more' always works.

o Or, 'And what happened next?'

o Or even 'How come?', which is a softer version of 'Why do you do that?'. But it could mean, for example, 'How did you get into that line of work?'. 'How come?' is a top question: whenever anybody says anything, just ask, 'How come?'. They are bound to tell you something they weren't going to tell you otherwise. And it's a much better formulation than 'Why?', which seems to demand a scientific explanation of all the reasons, whereas 'How come?' just moves it along nicely.

o Empathise. 'That must be fascinating/easy/troublesome/ boring/lucrative/impressive/'. All of these variants invite a response and, even if it is just 'Yes, it is', at least you've tried, and you can respond 'How come?'

o 'Tell me more' is good: very open and neutral.

o Or, 'because…?'. I've been told not to do this as it is allegedly perceived as aggressive; yet a gentle 'because…?' just encourages the speaker to continue.

o Or, even 'mmmm…' hummed sympathetically. You might have to practise that if you want to give the impression that your request is the result of a weighty decision-making process. (Psychotherapists are very good at it, if you happen to know any.)

The point is that no-one will tell you anything interesting within one minute of meeting you for the first time in their lives (unless they are flagrant exhibitionists). But, after three or four minutes where they have been gently encouraged to stick to a single topic, they might reveal something interesting. This is not 'manipulation', with or without the quotation marks. This is having a conversation.

It cannot be the case that, at the time, you know what they say will be fruitless, so plug on with it.

I have been to a networking dinner where, sitting next to someone, escape was impossible, and where, having said I work with EI, the whole conversation was then about me and my business. Try as I might, I couldn't get him to talk about himself or his business. Conversely, with someone else, I started by asking about their business and the subject never veered from it in thirty solid minutes. You just have to accept other people for what they are, having let go of your expectations.

77 Good answers to give

As we discussed in section 8, the answer to the question 'What do you do?' shouldn't be 'I do…'. The simplest, most coherent way to do this is to answer with:

o 'May I answer that by telling a story?'

And, off you go with all the stuff in that section.

What people at networking events want—or at least are immensely relieved and receptive if you provide it—is to be entertained, to be amused, to be mildly surprised. If your story is structured well, it will have hooks that allow the other person to ask, 'Blimey, how did you do that?' You should always answer in ways that emphasise the wisdom of the client in employing you above your wisdom in sorting out their problem.

To interrupt a conversation, go up to the people and say, 'May I interrupt you [please]?' As previously noted, networking events are not forums for holding private conversations, so you are positively helping these people to stop being anti-social.

Extricating yourself from a conversation is a two-step process:

Step 1: the immediate future. 'I really must circulate/move around the room/talk to some more people/speak to the tame gorilla I saw in the corner'. All of these will be received with total understanding and, possibly, relief from the other person who wishes they'd thought of saying it ages ago.

Step 2: looking slightly further into the future. 'Look, it was a pleasure/it was fascinating/enlightening/interesting talking to you. Let's get together and have a one-to-one follow-up meeting.' You exchange cards and you fix the meeting via email on your return to the office.

If you feel a follow-up is inappropriate, just say something along the lines, of 'Look, it was a pleasure/etc talking to you'. Stop there, and move into the 'I really must circulate…' bit. Closing remarks like 'Have a nice life' probably won't go down well.

How long you leave it before playing this card depends on how well you are getting on in the conversation. If it's going hesitatingly, follow the advice in *Macbeth*:

> If it were done when 'tis done, then 'twere well
> It were done quickly…

If it is going well, still terminate the conversation quickly: you definitely want to have a follow-up meeting with this person.

The bottom line is that you are in a room with fifteen or fifty other people. You should be having brief conversations with lots of them and following up with the promising ones some other time.

78 Listening is more important than talking

What stops us from listening well?

Effective and flexible networkers are also good listeners. Listening with care is a skill. Many people degrade the quality of their listening—or stop altogether—by:

a Interrupting—when we interrupt, it can be because we don't respect the other's contribution to the conversation and want to put our interests first.

b Thinking ahead—what are we going to say next? This is of course intended to meet our need to continue what we last said, not to pay attention to what the other person is currently saying and give them a useful response.

c Disagreeing with the other person, judging them and otherwise measuring or evaluating them.

d Thinking about what to have for dinner later—and generally allowing one's mind to wander.

e Being distracted by extraneous noises, conversations and things going on in peripheral vision.

Be aware of how much you do some of these, and practise focussing on the other person instead. If you make the other person more important than you, it will be easier not to fall into these traps that are all ways in which we make ourselves more important than them.

Listen to understand. Listening has a purpose beyond the development of rapport, of course. We listen in order to understand the other person. With the best will in the world, though, we don't always understand what they mean, so we need to communicate our need to understand more.

79 Dealing with difficult people

In the short, somewhat superficial encounters we have at networking events, or even at one-to-one follow-up meetings, it's unlikely we shall find out just how difficult some people can be given enough time and space. Nevertheless, it's worth running through just two of the many principles that are worth bearing in mind.

Story: The dreaded Freda

Years ago, I had a job in a rather civil service-like office. There was a manager, Freda, whom everyone felt was a pain in the neck. She was difficult. She managed half the office and she seemed always to be bearing down on them, never cutting them any slack and generally behaving like a minor despotic ruler.

Everyone, without exception, whether they reported to her or to the other manager in the office, would have said she was a difficult person.

Everyone, that is, except one person: Roger. Roger had Freda around his little finger. Not only did Roger not feel that Freda was a difficult person, she wasn't a difficult person in her work relationship with him, full stop.

The first rule is 'It's their stuff'.

If someone is behaving in a difficult way, it's their stuff. In some cases, there may have been a recent precipitating factor, such as an argument earlier in the day with someone; or they may have some chronic medical condition that gives them pain; or they have been rejected by *The X Factor*. It's true that they might have disguised these influences, or got over them, but they haven't done this well.

In other cases, it is unfortunately true that a person can just be a 'nasty piece of work', as my father used to say. It's almost arrogant to imagine that they are being difficult 'just for you'.

The second rule is 'It's your stuff'.

You've let them press your buttons. As in the case of Roger above, he communicated, however subconsciously, that he wasn't going to let Freda press his buttons. Maybe there had been a little standoff in the past, before I joined the team, and Roger had made his position clear in a way that Freda positively welcomed (Freda being surprisingly captivated by strong men with small moustaches).

The rule says, though, that if you had concealed those buttons a little better, or if you had decided you weren't going to have those buttons pressed at all, the other person wouldn't be able to press them. This is what Roger did.

Everyone else just used Freda as a generic scapegoat—the traditional 'difficult' person—a role that, admittedly, she appeared happy to play.

Think about what may be going on for them.

Their world may be full of problems: everything from a poor financial performance of the business to a difficult client; they may be anxious about something; they may be short of sleep; the cat might have run off with the milkman. People cannot stop their personal lives intruding into their business lives. And nor can we.

Consider that they are doing the best they can in the circumstances. OK, they might be able to do better with only a little more effort, but 'cut them some slack' as they say. Don't blame or judge them; respect them.

Maintain an adult approach that doesn't put them down. Blame and judgement, particularly the righteous sort, will always exacerbate the situation. Expressing such an attitude is only really about being right about the other person and making damn sure they know it.

80 Giving

People who are giving are attractive. I don't mean having a website that says 'Download my free sixteen-page book on internet marketing—once you've parted with some personal information'. That's selling. Giving is when someone expresses a need for something, preferably to your face, and you are able to help in some way. You give at least information, and possibly your time conducting a little research back at the office.

Offering a free book online is like the vendor of promotional toys handing out things people don't really want at networking events. I have something that such a company gave me. It sits on a little stand; it's a piece of metal inclined at 45 degrees with a sticky surface. I think you're supposed to place your mobile phone on it. However, it is too small for my phone, and the sticky stuff has never stuck, and I certainly didn't ask for it. It turns out to have no value other than to provide an example in this book. That's not giving either.

In any conversation, find out how you can help the other person. The easiest way to do this is to say, 'How can I help you?' A better way is possible if they have said something while you have chatted that indicated what they needed, maybe just a name, that you can give to them as you talk (or send them afterwards if you need to find it).

If I am at a networking event and I see someone who is a guest, I will often ask them if they are new to the organisation holding the event. If so, I will probably say, 'Do you mind if I tell you something that I have found useful here?' Nobody has ever minded. I tell them about connectors and mavens and why these people are helpful. I then tell them who the connectors and mavens are in the room at that moment and offer to introduce them. People say they find that helpful. It's the old principle that givers gain.

Beware of inauthenticity, 'giving in order to get', though (see **120**). You can usually tell if you are running that particular belief because you notice that you are always giving, but you don't get much back. If you need specific help that you think the other person can give, there's absolutely nothing wrong with asking for it.

III So, how come it's not working?

11 Follow the rules

81 Showing the way

Story: Troy

Three thousand years ago, dusk is falling. You are overlooking the plains of Troy, watching the Greek army encamped outside the city, the soldiers biding their time before they can take the city. A mysterious figure is moving from tent… to tent… to tent.

Who is he?

It is Agamemnon, the king. He is making sure that all his men are as comfortable as they can be under the circumstances and that they have the food and water they need. Only when he is satisfied he has done all he can for them does he go to his own tent to eat and sleep.

82 Make the other person more important than you

This is the 'leadership precept'.

Once more, I must stress that, although I home in on the 'networking event' as the forum in which you talk about your business, its products and services, and yourself, everything in the book is relevant in whatever context you are talking to others. This is more true than ever when it comes to the leadership precept.

Without a doubt, this is one of the most important topics in the book. But it has two unfortunate aspects:

a   Many people refuse to do it, or even just to experiment with it a little. This is partly because they misunderstand it (see (b)) and partly because it conflicts with the scarcity model they are running.

b   'Making the other person more important than you' is *not* believing that they *are* more important. It is acting *as if they were* more important than you.

The problem is that British people mistake this approach of *making the other person more important than you* for servility or subservience. Yet it is something else entirely: it is about being *in service*. It isn't a value judgement either on oneself or on the other person. It defines an *approach* to other people; it's an *approach* that turns out to be very useful if you want to work with someone.

An approach is a set of beliefs and feelings that work on each other to create a third thing: an attitude.

On the other hand, putting oneself in a position of servility would be the thin end of a very nasty wedge whose thick end is a victim/abuser relationship. Of course, many people *do* attempt to put others in an inferior position. Any business in which the concepts of superior and subordinate operate risks doing this and many go right ahead and just do it. But, in networking, where there is no need, and no possible justification, for one business person to think of another as inferior to them, it has no place.

This makes things awkward when someone in a networking group wants to be in a dependent position; wants the rest of the group to look after them. It can be hard to maintain a dispassionate stance towards them.

Making the other person more important than you is putting the needs of the other person before your needs. It takes off as a precept worth following when the other person reciprocates and makes you more important than *them*. As such it is an essential component of partnership, the real goal of all networking relationships.

At the Royal Military Academy, Sandhurst, where the British Army trains its officers and those of other countries, the motto is:

Serve to lead.

This says that, if you want to lead that squad of trained soldiers you need to be in service to them first. This is what Agamemnon was doing. There was no sense that Agamemnon thought that his soldiers were 'better' than him (or 'worse' for that matter); he just acted as if they were. This created the loyalty and motivation that are essential for leadership—and, of course, for productive networking.

Agamemnon is in this book to convince anyone who needs convincing that making the other person more important than them will not result in them being walked all over and exploited. In fact, when I talk about this at presentations to business people, I suggest that, if it is good enough for the British Army, it is at least worth them trying it.

Interestingly, in any semi-closed group such as those at a regular networking event, once one influential person in the group starts making other people more important than them (the organiser maybe, or a connector or maven—see **16**), some other people will start doing it as well. This is also a dynamic that military and other groups rely on for success: in other spheres it might be called 'comradeship'. It is relatively easy for this to become a cultural norm without anyone being really aware that they are contributing to it. People tend to match and follow others.

83 Deal with the world as it is, not as you would like it to be

This might be the ultimate precept in terms of its simplicity and obviousness, yet it can be the hardest to implement (but that's zen proverbs for you). Our awareness and understanding of the world is entirely mediated by our beliefs and thoughts, our emotions and feelings; by our capacities to perceive and understand; by our judgements and projections; and by our strengths and weaknesses.

So the world 'as it is' for me is not going to be the same as the world 'as it is' for you, even if we both honestly believe we are perceiving the same bits of the world at any one time.

When our world is temporarily the networking event, we need a strategy to be at the event in a way that, as well as we can, respects what's actually going on, not what we would like to have going on. What we would like is, no doubt, other people to be interesting and engaging, we'd like lots of leads spontaneously given and we'd like a decent meal. The reality is that, if we want these things, we shall probably have to be the person delivering them.

More widely, we want the world to be a certain way—that we have enough clients, we are successful at networking, our business is revered by our peers, people admire us and so on— and we get upset when we discover that it isn't quite that way. We have difficulty not because it's so much a *belief* that the world is a certain way that is the problem. It is an *expectation* that this is so. And, as expectations are usually dressed-up demands, we are essentially frustrated that our demands that the world be a certain way aren't being met. Because the world is out of our control, this frustration is inevitable.

Until we see the situation for what it really is, we have no chance of defining and then carrying out those tasks needed to bring our world to where we want it to be. We are using the frustration as a block to move forward. However, when we do decide to move forward, we risk hitting that other problem, our resistance to change.

84 Be the change you want to see in the world

This well-known saying attributed to Mahatma Gandhi encapsulates one of the most important ways of being. We cannot expect others to do something if we aren't prepared to do it ourselves. This applies as equally to the international renunciation of nuclear weapons as it does to our work relationships.

What we see missing is what we are called to give. If something needs to be done, it is useful if we take responsibility for doing it ourselves. It improves the general good. If we can't carry out the action, we need to find someone who can.

Firstly, it is a good counter to the often less than sparkling networking events we are offered as business people. If there's something missing, or could be done better, at least tell the organisers and, preferably, offer to do something about it.

Just think how much your standing in the group will rise if you do this. (Particularly if you happen to mention, nicely, to a few people that you were responsible for the change from which they are now all benefitting.) You will be seen as a proactive person who gets things done. You will gain a positive reputation in the group, at least for a time, and you will have the opportunity to capitalise on that.

Secondly—and I find this all the time in one-to-one meetings—many business people are unlikely to intuit the process of developing networking relationships, and what their role is in doing this. If we expect to move a relationship with a business person from a state of awareness (at best) to one where real benefits are being given and received by both parties, it would be best to assume that we have to follow Gandhi. We have to be those things that are required if the relationship is going to progress. For a start, we have to make the other person more important than us. It is unlikely that the other person will do this if the idea has never occurred to them.

85 Seek to understand the other person

Many people assume that other people think and feel just like they do, without stopping to consider whether that is the case.

How we see another person is largely dependent on the intention we set for our relationship with them, and often this is done unconsciously. Try instead to set the intention consciously, since this is the level at which we can influence the relationship most easily. We can choose to see any relationship as a vehicle for learning, growth and mutual success. With this attitude, we will naturally want to understand the other person, being curious as to what there is for us to learn.

How do they approach business? What do they see as success? Why are they talking to you?

It's worth entertaining the belief that there is no situation between two or more people in which there is too much communication. There may be too much noise and handwaving, but that isn't communication. Likewise in our conversations with those we meet at networking events, we must be harsh and see that a lot of noise is going on. But is anything actually being communicated? Of that, what is useful?

It is the quality of the communication that is important. This is a real stumbling block to the development of strong business relationships (just as it is a stumbling block to the development of strong personal ones).

Set your intention not only to see the world from their shoes, but also to see it as *they* do from their shoes.

86 Let go of the need to be right

Story: Sacrifice

Damian owned a successful consultancy business. He was, to be sure, a bit of a 'control freak' but, on the whole, he was reasonably judicious in deciding which things to be controlling about and which things to leave to the consultants' choices.

He was absolute, however, in his insistence that all consultants charge the same daily fee rate, irrespective of the job, the client, the client's market sector, their location or anything else. While it is a good idea to have a consistent business model applied across all consultants, the problem here was that Damian's stipulated fee was too high for the market to bear and the consultants, particularly those outside London, couldn't get any clients.

No clients meant no cut for Damian and no profit for the central business. Yet Damian was deaf to all entreaties to discount the price, however often they were repeated. In the end, many of the consultants left and found something else to do.

*I would go so far as to say that Damian would rather have
sacrificed his business than admit he had been wrong about
the fee rate.*

When I say, 'let go of the need to be right', I am certainly
not advocating being wrong. What I am suggesting is that an
attachment to being right, a *need* to be right such as Damian had,
will not serve you or the business.

Someone who has a strong need to be right is probably deaf
to ideas, thoughts and suggestions about the business that
come from others, particularly if these ideas are perceived to
be criticism. Yet all businesses thrive when there is plenty of
contribution from those in it and outside it. They thrive when
there is rational conversation between people who do not feel
their position will be threatened by their point of view being
rejected before it is even spoken. Being right all the time is
not only unendearing, it shows a closed mind—a refusal to
communicate—and tends to push people away (which is
what Damian ended up doing to all the consultants he had
spent some considerable time and expense bringing into his
business). This can increase a sense of isolation that some
small-business people have.

Insisting on being right means we lose opportunities to learn
and grow, and we risk giving in or giving up, even if assistance
is just a phone call away, because the perceived cost of changing
one's mind is too great.

And, if it turns out that someone really is wrong, as Damian was
in his case, then it can be problematic: no amount of advising
him to deal with the world as it is and not how he would like
it to be will help. He may well see the truth in this maxim yet
still be caught in this trap of his own making, so powerful may
be his need to be right.

It is an unfortunate aspect of our work culture that 'being right'
is seen as a good thing. (This also applies to most domains in
our society, starting with politics.) It is worth fighting this
attitude that sticking to your guns—despite all the evidence
that a contrary position would be more helpful—is a sign of
strength or leadership when it is nothing of the sort. At its
extreme, a whole country can be devastated by the mad ideas
of that most pernicious of beasts, a 'conviction politician'.

87 Feel the anxiety, and do it anyway

In 1987, Susan Jeffers published her book, *Feel the Fear and Do It Anyway*®. Such a good title. Except that it is not about fear. It's about anxiety, and fear and anxiety aren't the same thing. But I guess that *Feel the anxiety and do it anyway* just doesn't have the same ring.

Fear is an *instinct*. An instinct is an innate predisposition to behave in certain ways following certain stimuli. By 'innate' I mean it seems to be 'prewired': we appear to be born with it and, in particular, it isn't learnt. By 'predisposition' I mean that the response—in this case fear—is more likely to be displayed in some types of situation (fierce, hungry lion rushing for your throat) than others (fluffy kitten trying to chew your socks).

Anxiety is a *feeling*, a feeling propelled by the behaviour called 'worry'. We worry that something *could* be the case— for example, that people will find us boring at networking events—and this worry gives rise to a feeling of anxiety. We then turn up at a networking event anxious as hell. We trip over our words and we are obviously nervous. We communicate poorly, or we avoid communicating at all, preferring to find a plate of flagging sausage rolls suddenly of compelling interest. Inevitably, we end up being perceived as being boring by everyone else. The big question is, to what extent does it *suit* us that that is the case? Because, if there is no 'benefit', at some level, from doing it, we wouldn't do it.

If we see that lion bounding towards us, its open jaws slavering and aimed straight at our throat, we experience fear. The fear instinct compels us to run away or climb a lamppost—it's triggered at an entirely subconscious level. If we are strolling down a street in Orpington, worried that a lion *might* bound towards us, its open jaws slavering, etc, then we are experiencing anxiety.

Because anxiety is a feeling, we can consciously do something about it. That's the point, and the point of Jeffers' book. We can choose to believe that the thing we worry will happen is highly unlikely to happen. We can choose to believe that, even if it did happen (for example, people find us boring at networking events):

○ we can cope with it—which we can
○ we can modify our behaviour 'in real time' to adjust to the feedback we are getting
○ we can learn from it.

So, because we are talking about a feeling, not an instinct, we can choose to feel something else.

The story of Maggie is an example of this. Maggie chose to replace her belief that she would humiliate herself at any networking event with a belief that she could handle a few brief, superficial conversations, even with people she didn't know. She chose to believe that she could handle the possibly one or two embarrassing moments that occurred (which she could have done had they happened).

Story: Slimming class

For some reason lost in the mists of time, I felt the urge to join a slimming class a few years ago. There I was, definitely outside my comfort zone, trying to pay attention to what 'teacher' was telling us. She was doing well, I thought. Having more than a passing interest in how trainers work, I was entirely satisfied with her performance until well past the mid-session break. At which point, for some unaccountable reason, she chose to share with us that this was her first ever class as a 'teacher' and she was rather nervous. I felt like crying out, 'For heaven's sake, don't say that!'. It had been entirely unnecessary because:

○ it was way past the time she should have worried about building a rapport with the class, which she had done successfully earlier
○ she was doing just fine.

I don't think anyone either suspected or cared whether it was her first time or not. But from that point on, everyone was out to spot a slip-up (in a nice supportive way, of course).

There's a lot to be said for 'acting as if', providing it is done authentically. In this case, authentically means not just 'going through the motions', but giving it your best shot, keeping in mind the injunction to 'make the other person more important than you'.

Anyway, Maggie chose to replace her anxiety with at least a little confidence that she could get through it. Just as with my experience with the Alsatians, a very little confidence grew and grew, fed by the positive experience that she, to her surprise, was having at networking events. As she became increasingly confident, she was able to do more at events and to attend more events. Eventually, she started assisting with the organisation of events. She created a virtuous spiral to the point that you couldn't keep her away from them in the end! And my slimming class trainer did just fine over all her sessions. I even lost some weight and was a star pupil one week (it took me straight back to when Mrs Jones gave me a gold star at primary school).

Anxiety is the experience of apprehension we feel at the threat of being moved out of our comfort zone. Outside our comfort zone is a 'stretch zone': as it happens, this is where we need to be. This is not a place of stress; it is a place of adrenalin, maybe, and of some constructive tension. But, the more times we visit it, the more comfortable we are in it. Before we know it, our comfort zone has extended into that area, pushing the stretch zone further back.

Of course, once one has felt the anxiety and done it anyway, there is just something else we have to feel the anxiety about. And so on. C'est la vie.

88 The meaning of a communication is what the recipient makes of it

This apparently perverse principle is worth sticking with. If I think I am saying something clear, unambiguous and precise, but you 'misunderstand' it, your 'misunderstanding' is the message you take from my communication. It's the only possible message you could possibly take. You aren't a mind reader, after all!

So, the more carelessly you express something, the more likely it is that the other person will get a different message from the one you intend them to get. Of course, sometimes, they just end up confused—but that's presumably not what you intended either.

It gets more complicated. A part of any communication is subconscious: we are unaware of that part. Subconscious communication is typically non-verbal: it may be that I used a tone of voice that I wasn't aware of. You felt something was incongruent. You didn't *explicitly* register that the tone of voice was at odds with the words, but you still picked it up. That incongruity is, itself, a message. Similarly, you might notice an incongruity through my choice of particular words, or my gestures. It could lie in what was *not* said and so on.

Even when you are aware of the non-verbal content of the communication, it is tricky to pin down. But nevertheless, the listener puts everything they've received, consciously and subconsciously, into the message they create from someone's communication.

If my communication requires you to know or understand something that you just don't know, you will make assumptions. You will substitute what you do know, if you can, and understand as best you can. Again, this is partly a subconscious process, so you are not aware you are doing it.

If the recipient appears not to understand what you just said to them in what you thought were such nice simple terms, it's not surprising. I say 'appears' because how would you know that they hadn't grasped what you said if they didn't communicate that fact to you in some way? But, if they do that, the same process kicks in. This time you cannot but pick up the effects of subconscious and non-verbal components, and apply your interpretations and assumptions to what they say!

So, we cannot be sure what they 'really meant' when they were telling us they weren't sure what we really meant. Or, in the immortal words of Frank Zappa:

> *Just because somebody hears something you say, or reads something that you write, doesn't mean you've reached them.*

Story: Thatcher

A classic example of this phenomenon happened following the then prime minister Margaret Thatcher's reported statement (in Woman's Own, 1987) that 'There is no such thing as society'. Although her apologists to this day insist she was quoted out of context and she meant something else entirely, the message that most people got (and which flooded the media for months, if not years) was, in fact, 'There is no such thing as society'.

89 We already have all the resources we need

This is a belief. Is it true? Not invariably, I am sure. But is it a useful belief to hold? I think, yes, because it is a counter to the excuse, 'I can't do this because I don't have X' (as in 'I can't go to the networking event because I haven't prepared enough stories'). Of course, there are hundreds of millions of people on the planet who do not have all the resources they need right now, such as enough food. I don't want to belittle their plight with what some could accuse of being a first-world, middle-class problem. However, within the context of the people reading this book about business networking, it's hard to argue that we don't have all have the resources we need in order to make a good impression on others.

At worst, this **principle** may need to be slightly modified: 'We already have all the resources we need right now'. If some part of our networking endeavour is clearly unachievable now, at least we have the resources now to obtain what we shall need in the future.

90 There is no failure, only feedback

This sentiment, much beloved of NLP practitioners, is a classic example of a belief you can choose to hold or not. It's up to you. The only reason for holding the belief is that it is helpful. We might return from a networking event believing we have 'messed up': we didn't tell a story well, it rambled and the punchline was wrong; we failed to seek out some self-evidently interesting people to talk to; we made our lack of interest in someone else's business all too apparent; we spilt gravy on our blouse; and that's just the half of it. We can sit and sulk and, at worst, resolve never to go to another networking event. Or we can listen to the feedback we are giving ourselves:

a   We can revise our stories, making them snappier, and we can practise telling them.

b   We can research the guest list of the next event better, make a point of talking to the most interesting people, asking the organiser to introduce us if we don't recognise the other person. Ask the organiser who the most interesting people are, if necessary. (And, if we end up not meeting them, we can send them a message afterwards to the effect, 'we were at the same event on Tuesday but unfortunately didn't have a chance to talk. Do you have twenty minutes for a conversation over the phone?').

c   We can set an intention before we go into the next event that we will place our interest in the other person and then stick to it.

d   We can use our napkin next time.

Apart from anything else, a willingness to come back after a perceived failure—to show up again—is an attractive characteristic (though, remember, only you really thought it was a failure, an embarrassment, or even noticed). There's enough in this book about letting go of attachments to being right (see **86**) for us to understand how unattractive that attachment is, and someone who shows they have learnt from experience is someone others should want to get to know.

The idea that we can attend an event and make no mistakes, or do nothing that, on reflection, we believe we couldn't have done better, is unrealistic. The only way we could do that is by doing nothing. But doing nothing is definitely a mistake! Learn from mistakes: the mistakes tell you what you need to learn. Then do it differently or better next time.

As Leo Buscaglia wrote in Living, Loving and Learning:

> To try is to risk failure, but risks must be taken, because the greatest hazard in life is to risk nothing.

91   Curiosity is more useful than expectation

Try this little exercise:

Get a bunch of keys. Pretend that they are a fragile and valuable object that, for now, represents some of your cherished beliefs and expectations of others. Hold the keys in one hand, close your fingers, making a fist over them and then hold out that fist at arm's length, with the back of your hand uppermost. This represents holding onto your beliefs and expectations. You know that, were you to open your hand, the keys would drop to the floor. Your precious, fragile beliefs and expectations would crash to the floor and shatter, and part of you may be destroyed forever. We do not want this to happen, so we hold on tightly to the keys (that is, to our beliefs and expectations).

So, open your fist and let go of the keys. Your precious, fragile beliefs and expectations crash to the floor and shatter, just as you knew they would.

Pick up the keys and start again. Hold the keys in one hand, make a fist over them and hold out that hand at arm's length, with your fingers uppermost. Once again, this represents you holding onto your beliefs and expectations. Open your fist. What happens? The keys stay put. Your precious, fragile beliefs and expectations are still there in the palm of your hand. They are still part of you. But you're not attached to them: you aren't clinging on to them.

Replace the expectations with curiosity. As humans, if we let go of something, we need something else to hold on to, something to fill that space. I recommend something that has served me and many others well. It is simple curiosity. Set an intention that you will be curious.

Be curious about what happens when you go to a networking event you are anxious about. Be curious about what people will say; curious about what someone would say if you said X; curious about how well you will respond when asked what you do. Be curious about whether there is someone at the event who knows someone who might be interested in your services; curious about how you can help them. And, of course, be curious about what's for lunch.

This works as a tactic because curiosity is a powerful thing. It is a motivating approach because, even if we are not invested in the outcome, we can simply be curious to find out what happens next.

92 Be present

Simply means, firstly, be there physically. Turn up. Woody Allen is said to have said:

> 80 percent of success is showing up.

Don't believe that 'Networking is something I can do when I haven't anything better in the diary' (see **16**). And, once you are there, be mentally present too. Pay attention to what others are saying and be interested in them in real time. Don't let your mind wander. It's annoyingly true that people can pick up a lack of presence (just as you can). Be aware that being distant—emotionally and mentally—can be interpreted as passive aggression.

12 Improve your approach

93 Introduction

Just as the athlete or musician does their final warm-ups before they have to perform, so it is useful for the networker to do the same. It is all about seeing networking as a real job and, for the novice, there is plenty to practise. It's about recognising that contributing well to a networking event is as valuable to your business as contributing well to a client.

Most of what follows in this section is about beliefs, feelings, approaches and attitudes. Given that networking is standing in a room talking to people, it is quite hard to come up with a lot of behavioural tips, though there is plenty to say about what you should be preparing to say. Let me add these two suggestions to the topics that follow:

o   trust your intuition

o   be confident.

Trust your intuition. Intuition is not some mysterious intestinal by-product. It is simply unconscious rationality, so go with what it tells you. It can be expressed as a feeling: 'I have a strong feeling I should...', though what happens is that the idea just 'pops into your head'. That's your intuition talking. The reason that it is called 'gut reaction' or whatever, is that many mental processes are accompanied by bodily feelings and, I guess, the intestines are a popular location for intuition.

Anyway, call it what you like, you know it, you've known it all your life, and it is worth heeding.

Of course, intuition is not always right, though the speed with which insights come to you could make you think it was. But nor is it some random outpouring, either.

Be confident. Act 'as if' if necessary. As the slimming class story shows (see **87**), people will assume you are confident unless you let them discover you aren't. If you *'act as if' authentically*, there's no harm in it. And, before you know it, you will have taught yourself what being confident feels like and, given no reason not to be, you will just be confident. End of.

Martin Davies, of NRG Networks, has been an observer and facilitator of over a thousand networking events. He was unequivocal when I asked him what networkers' weak spots are:

o 'not making themselves sufficiently attractive', and

o 'their need goes before their ability to give. Too needy.'

It is surprising how high up the list Davies puts neediness. His opinion is worth listening to. One of the themes of this book is about being attractive. Neediness is never attractive. The person who is attracted to you is ten times more motivated to work with you than the one you have thrust yourself upon.

Sarah Owen, formerly of Asentiv, has trained many people to be better networkers. I asked her what she felt were the principal weak spots of trainees before she had got her hands on them. It's worth quoting her answer in full:

'What I have learned is that people's weak spots are usually tied to their behavioural styles. If I had to say, the most common on that basis are:

o *Arrogance*—people who don't think they have anything to learn on the topic.

o *Talking a lot!*—people who talk too much and don't always remember to follow up.

o *Not talking enough!*—people who don't talk enough; both these tend to lead to a lack of clarity in their message or purpose.

o *Too earnest!*—people who overthink it and make it too complicated, or are too guarded and don't open their hearts to people which, after all, is a key ingredient needed to build relationships.'

Owen speaks from a more behavioural point of view than I do. Having been trained by her and her colleagues, I can attest to the need for this approach. It complements, rather than contradicts, the current book.

94 You think the process is behavioural—but it isn't

Much of business is procedural and it is possible to determine the best procedures to achieve almost any end. 'Procedure' means rational, 'thinking' processes; processes untainted by the apparent irrationality of emotions and instinct.

However, less of business is procedural than some business people would like to believe. And that is, of course, because businesses are just people or, as I prefer to say, a business is just the sum of the relationships between the people in it and between them and those the business touches.

It's a good idea to assume that the behavioural aspects of networking are so straightforward that the only things worth spending time cultivating are the emotional and intuitive aspects. This is not least because, if you sort them out, the behavioural stuff will improve if it has to. Sort out the reasons why people appear to find you uninteresting and you will be a different person: an interesting person.

There are a number of reasons why people fight shy of considering feelings and intuition in business.

Feelings and intuition are perceived to be unpredictable. But they aren't. Firstly, feelings and intuition are not the same thing. Feelings can be anticipated successfully, otherwise the vast cadre of therapists, counsellors, coaches and the rest of us wouldn't have a chance. Most people will respond emotionally in the same way as everyone else to a given situation. Each person will almost certainly respond in the same way to similar situations they encounter. Feelings are predictable enough.

Intuition is a *rational*, but subconscious, process. So its unpredictability, if that is what it is, is largely due to its invisibility. Dan Ariely in his book, predictably titled *Predictably irrational*, gives many examples of situations where people, acting on feelings and intuition, behave predictably.

Feelings and intuition are perceived to be unmeasurable. That's true but irrelevant. According to the Drucker Institute, Peter Drucker didn't say—contrary to widespread belief—'If you can't measure it, you can't manage it'. Just as well, because that is self-evidently silly.

'*We don't go there.*' The two points above are usually the reasons (read excuses) why some people—and they are not all male by any means—don't 'do' emotions, they 'don't go there'. In truth, we are all reluctant to a greater or lesser degree to expose our emotions, particularly in contexts (such as business) where we don't know, let alone trust, all the people in the room.

My suggestion is to push yourself into your stretch zone, as described in **29**. Don't push so far that you stress yourself by worrying that you will be mortally embarrassed, couldn't bear the indignity of it and couldn't handle your responses or anyone else's indignity. But, just push yourself a little. The reward is that people will see that as openness (because it is), and people find openness in others attractive.

The behavioural aspects of networking are by the by. Much of this book is about what to do. Of course networking is behavioural. But that is a veneer. The point is what is going on underneath in order for you to do it. The emotional and intuitive responses are what you need to offer, and what you need to get from others, if the whole thing is going to work. It's precisely the opposite of what most people think: that is, that the emotional and intuitive stuff is the veneer that colours the behaviour.

95 You're kidding yourself

You think you are making it about the other person when actually you are making it about you.

> Story: No-one helps me
>
> Karen was complaining to me, at a networking event, as it happens, that she was 'very good' at seeking out ways to help

others and then delivering on her undertakings. But no-one ever asked her how they could help her.

Here are three answers:

a It is like Rachel who complained that no-one ever invited her to a one-to-one (**114**): other people don't always 'get it', and the best that Rachel and Karen can hope for is to be seen, however subconsciously, as leaders who influence others. You can bet that at least some of the people they help will get the message and go on to adopt this practice themselves.

b Karen wants to be dependent on others when, actually, she needs to show up and take the lead. See below.

c Karen was deluding herself. She really found it difficult to ask for help, seeing it as a weakness.

Giving in order to get is the most likely explanation. It is a classic tactic of those who have a suppressed expectation of getting something in return for their favours. 'Why shouldn't I get something in return?' The irony is that you are more likely to get something if you don't demand it than if you do. People do give willingly, particularly to those who have given to them. A belief that it isn't going to happen unless you demand it is really a belief that no-one would want to give to you unless you had obligated them. And that's a symptom of low self-esteem and/or the scarcity model.

(Of course, the opposite—'I'm such a wonderful person that everyone should shower me with gifts'—is also a demand, and more insufferable, too. Happily, it is rarer—at least in the UK.)

Everybody does this, but some people reconcile more successfully than others the conflicting demands of helping others and looking after themselves. Consider the difference between purpose and intention. **47** looked at this in detail. Essentially, there are differences between one's purpose in doing something and one's intention in doing it.

For example, Tracey goes to a regular networking event. Her *purpose* is to find people she can help such that the *outcomes* are that they help her back. She sets herself an *intention* to talk to at least six people there, two of whom she hasn't spoken to before. So purposes are definitely long term, outcomes probably so. But intentions apply to the event itself: they are *action* targets. They aren't expectations (those hidden demands we make of ourselves). Tracey gets a big tick for getting all her ducks in a row.

So, if you go to an event with the purpose of seeing if you can help others, you will find that that underlying purpose affects what you say to people and even who you choose to speak to. It will define what you do after the event, in terms of any commitments you might have made to people ('I'll look up that article when I get back to the office and email it to you').

You will have previously thought through your purpose and outcomes, so you will be confident that, if you do the things you need to do to achieve the purpose, the outcomes should follow. You enter the event with intentions to speak to at least ten people, get their business cards, ask each of them who else they know…

The business cards will enable you to invite people to one-to-one meetings, some of those invited will accept, the conversations at those one-to-ones may be more wide ranging and so on. So, by setting your intentions (action targets) at the start, you can ensure you do enough to achieve progress in the development of your business by helping others.

Another way of looking at this is to say that, in an event of thirty people, you can't talk to everyone, you can't offer to help everyone. So you choose to talk to the people who are most aligned with your business needs. In fact, a good intention would be to find those people first (however many, or few, there are).

When showing up and taking the lead, a useful precept is:

> *What you see is missing is what you are called to give.*

It's cousin to the precept attributed to Gandhi, 'Be the change you want to see in the world'.

One of the possible explanations of Karen's predicament is that she would really like to be in a dependent position and have people deliver clients and success to her on a plate. This works, if you can set it up right. When I was a business consultant, that was indeed my employer's business model. I just hung around waiting for the sales team to find me some work. As they were good at their job, and I was a model of compliant obedience, I wasn't hanging around much, but I didn't have much choice who I worked for.

However, in the world of small businesses, that approach isn't possible. Staying dependent can come across as needy (definitely a turn-off). A brittle, somewhat insincere exterior of helpfulness just adds to the difficulties others have with that approach. Better to stop being needy. A good way of doing that is to shut up about it and find some people in a worse situation than you—and help them.

But Karen may be stuck in independence, and that is no more useful a place to be than dependence. People there often refuse to let go of various beliefs around the scarcity model (**32**: 'you've got to do it all yourself', 'no-one will really help me, so why should I help them?', 'I haven't got the time and resources to waste on others' and so on). This is partly about needing to be right (see **86**).

If she's not careful, Karen will create a situation in which her belief that she has to do everything for herself will be her downfall because, actually, she can't do everything for herself.

So Karen needs to set an intention to be prepared to move outside her comfort zone, not into stress, but into her stretch zone. This will prepare her for becoming interdependent. In the medium and long term, she will have to find someone to be interdependent with, but it would be an excellent start if she nurtured those personal characteristics that make up interdependence. It's where she needs to be if she is going to develop successful business relationships and get referrals from them.

96 Fixing your purpose and outcomes

The most common mistake people make when defining their purpose in going to a networking event is being satisfied with an outcome for a purpose. Go back over **31** and see if your purpose isn't really an outcome. Even if you want your purpose in networking to be an outcome, maybe a different purpose is more realistic, achievable or useful.

The story of Jack's business in **35** shows that a helpful way of defining the purpose of a business is as solving a problem or problems that clients have. Transferring that thinking to networking, then, a useful purpose of going to a networking event is *to help others solve their issues*. I proposed this in **11** and explained why, far from just being a waste of time doing stuff for others without apparently making any progress looking after your own interests, it is an excellent way of making progress looking after your own interests.

If you don't trust that others will do this for you, it may be that the issue is not that all these people aren't trustworthy, but rather that you don't trust people (see **128**).

97 Fixing your intentions

What do you intend to have happen at the event? **47** explains that intentions aren't purposes or outcomes. Intentions can be very specific to a given event. They can be expressed in ways such as, 'I intend to get the names of three people I don't know whom I may be able to help'. Or, as in my case at the moment, my intention is to see how many introductions to publishers I can get from the people at the next meeting I attend.

You have to understand how specific intentions will contribute to achieving your purpose. If they don't contribute to your purpose, but feel right, does the purpose need adjusting?

How you set your intentions will determine what you do at the event (see the following topics). So, if they aren't doable, they will need modification, at least for the event in hand. Intentions are very helpful because, by the end of an event, even if you have only partially achieved your intention, you will have resources you didn't have a couple of hours ago that you can work with immediately to further your business.

For most cases, a good enough intention is to acquire the contact details of three people who have agreed, at the networking event, to have a one-to-one with you. But you can have more than one intention so, if you need to find a caterer, put that on the list, too.

98 Fixing your expectations

Expectations can be tricky because people use the word to mean different things.

The expectations I am talking about here are those that we impose on other people or organisations. We go to a networking event expecting there to be people who will help us, or even be clients. We expect someone to be useful without our asking them to do something. We expect someone to be helpful if we do ask them. We hope that people know, in some, undefined, way, what we need. In every case, we are disappointed. **48** goes through all of this in detail.

Of course, if you are paying to attend a networking event, you should be entitled to expect that it is run properly and delivers the goods and to complain when it doesn't. It is not, after all, difficult to run a networking event. However, life being what it is, one is disappointed. So, to avoid that, it's better to drop any expectations and approach the whole thing with curiosity, having set an intention or two. The more skilfully you can deploy a myriad of successful networking techniques, the less dissatisfied you will be with the event.

Many of us are prone to having expectations of ourselves only to beat ourselves up afterwards when we decide that we didn't meet them. (Possibly, in some cases, so that we can beat ourselves up.) Although that can be a tricky one to deal with, in a business context there is a way of addressing it.

Assume that one of your long-term expectations of yourself is that you always fulfil your intentions successfully. So, suppose you go to an event with an intention of talking to six people and yet you only speak to five. Ask yourself why.

Were you late and didn't have enough time? Were some people so interesting you spent 'too long' speaking to them? Whether it was really too long depends on what happens next, so it may well have been time well spent. If you are nervous about interrupting people who are talking to each other, don't be: networking events are not places to hold private meetings, and people shouldn't mind.

Some of these points seem to be too trite to mention here. Yet, it is over these little things that we become disappointed. We are very good at beating ourselves up for failing to meet our expectations of ourselves (again) rather than beating ourselves up (if we have to do that at all) for not getting to the bottom of what the problem is.

If you go to an event with the intention of inviting X people to one-to-one follow-ups and they all decline, consider inviting people by email next time, where you can explain in a little detail why you think it would be a good idea to meet. (I've never actually had this. I suspect that far too little inviting of people to one-to-ones goes on and anyone who actually gets an invitation is only too pleased.) If some people decline, so be it; they mark themselves by this act as people unlikely to be worth following up.

Expecting things of other people whom you don't know is just asking for trouble. The most common expectation is one that, sadly, is almost invariably dashed—particularly for the novice networker. This is that everyone else in the room must be really good at networking and one's own jejune attempts are to be rightly derided. They aren't and they won't be, in that order.

Everyone else has their own stuff, their own blocks and misunderstandings and, if you become halfway proficient, you will quickly rise to the top. Ironically, although I always advocate letting go of expectations because they do no good, in this sort of situation people probably expect too *little* of themselves compared with what they *could* achieve in a few months with only a little effort.

So, if your expectations are giving you difficulties, the simplest and best solution is to have none. (Recall that expecting nothing to happen is an expectation.) So, what if you think you *have* let go of your expectations, as the earlier piece advises? The answer is that, even though you have consciously done that, they are probably still there subconsciously, as with Karen (in **95**). Expectations are deeply ingrained in all of us and are a natural way of thinking.

The best solution is to consciously say to yourself that you will approach networking with an attitude of curiosity, and that it is your intention to do so. Write it down if necessary. Tell your friends, business colleagues, if necessary. Repeat it to yourself aloud ten times a day for a week (this is not a joke: affirmations work).

At this point many people become conflicted: they see the value of letting go of expectations, but they resist actually doing it. If this is you, assume that there is a part of you that is sticking up for having expectations and it needs to be reassured that you know what you are doing by seeking to abandon them. Speak to it. If necessary, out loud and, if necessary, more than once. Say, 'Thank you for looking out for my welfare, but I know that I do not need the expectations so please let go of them' (this is not a joke; it works).

99 Fixing your beliefs

'There's no use trying,' [Alice] said. 'One can't believe impossible things.'

'I daresay you haven't had much practice,' said the Queen. 'When I was your age, I always did it for half-an-hour a day. Why, sometimes I've believed as many as six impossible things before breakfast.'

(Lewis Carroll, Through the Looking-Glass)

Luckily, all the things I suggest you believe are both believable and useful!

Remind yourself of the principles and precepts of networking in the appendices. Pick a couple at random and be curious about how applying them will help you. Be curious why you chose those two.

The great thing about beliefs is that they are, well, beliefs. They are not inviolable truths. So, even if you wouldn't agree to hold a new belief for the rest of your life, you may be prepared to give it a whirl and see how you got on with it for two hours. And if you came to no great harm by doing so—and, indeed, you found it a curiously useful experience—you could consider holding that belief for two weeks or two months.

The principles and precepts are examples of ideas that it is useful to believe. Of course, you will hold many of these already—but do you action them as well as you could? Of the others, choose the one or two that you least like the idea of, or that you are the most sure will be a waste of time, and work with them. Your reservations about acting on those beliefs (which are, of course, only beliefs themselves) usually indicate an underlying reluctance to get to grips with something. Enacting the belief is a good way of making progress.

100 Being more attractive

In **25**, I suggested three levels of attractiveness that someone can have. I suggest that these are precisely tied to the three levels of success you can have at a networking event:

a   Failure: no-one seemed interested, no-one warmed to what you had to say, people didn't seem to 'rate' you (see **15**).

b   Indifference: it was basically OK, people said the right things (sometimes), maybe someone accepted an invitation to a one-to-one, but indifference sums it up.

c   Success! People laughed at your jokes, asked intelligent questions, enthusiastically accepted requests for follow-up one-to-one meetings (or even invited you first!), and pressed their contacts on you, offering to introduce you to people they know who will help you.

What causes this markedly wide range of responses? You do. OK, if the networking group's pet rabbit died that morning, other people may be on a downer but, on the whole, *overwhelmingly* how you are determines how other people respond to you and therefore how they seem to be to you.

And, while there are many and varied ways to be compelling, acting out a set of beliefs is the easiest, because all you have to keep in mind is the question, 'How should I be in order to be consistent with such and such a belief?', as in, for example, 'How should I be in order to make the other person more important than me?'.

One belief could be, 'Telling stories makes me memorable'.

This is not even as hard as learning to drive, though it does require a little practice (and commitment: that is, believing another belief, namely that doing this is worthwhile). However, if you follow Stanislavsky, the acting teacher and theatre director, and act 'as if'—in other words, you act as if you believed these beliefs—provided you do it authentically, you will be successful.

101 You are anxious about the meeting

Who isn't? Or, shouldn't be? Networking events provide many opportunities for you to shine so, why not shine as well as you can? A bit of performance anxiety is in order. But, let's not let it run out of control.

a   Prepare well in the day or days before the event. You will be able to turn up confident you know what you are doing. See sections 6 and 7 with more than a nod to section 12.

b   However much you prepare, ultimately you can only improve through practice. So, keep a journal. After each event, review what happened. Be honest; write down the things you could have done better. But also write down the things you did well. Go back through this book and understand why what you did well worked, and learn how to adjust those things you feel you did less well.

c   Ask for help. Particularly if you are paying for the event, the organisers should be willing to introduce you to several relevant people there. If there is only one organiser there and they have to be on the desk to greet arrivals, still insist that they walk you to the person they suggest to talk to *and* explain to that person that you are worth them talking to. Anything less really isn't acceptable and, if more networkers were vociferous in complaining about the inadequate organisation of events, the more likely it would be that the events would improve.

d   Remember that some of the other people at the event are more anxious than you. That doesn't excuse you from not rising above your anxiety, but it can be nice to feel that 'we're all in this together'.

Remember the words of Seneca, writing in the first century CE:

> It is not because things are difficult that we do not dare, it is because we do not dare that they are difficult.

102 Handling nerves on the day

Stage fright is only to be expected and, as Maggie showed, occasionally it can be severe—but it is *always short lasting.*

If you are aware of a physical sense of anxiety or pressure:

a   *Take some deep breaths*

Stand still first and breathe in slowly and deeply. Hold the breath a couple of seconds and exhale slowly. Repeat six times.

b   *Ground yourself*

Stand or sit. Make sure your shoes are placed squarely on the floor (take those stilettos off, chaps). Imagine all your weight gradually sinking to your lower body and legs, even as you stand up tall and straight. You might even imagine a cord attached to the top of your head gently pulling it to the sky.

c   *Affirm*

Talk to yourself (aloud, if you are in a position to; for example, in the car on the way to an event). Although it sounds implausible, it is possible to talk oneself into different beliefs. If your belief is something like 'I can't go through with this', your affirmation could be, 'I have the resources to go through with this'. A more generic affirmation could be 'I am a strong and resourceful person'.

Keep it short, don't be specific to individual tasks, and definitely state it positively and in the present tense. You might have to say it ten times; you might have to say it ten times every day for a fortnight. This is hardly onerous or difficult and well worth trying.

'Be early, leave last' sounds obvious but, if you don't want to enter a crowded room full of people you don't know, get there first. Then they all have to enter a room with you already in it. Plus, it offers you the chance to chat to whoever is hosting the event so you can make sure that you get an introduction, face to face, to someone worth talking to and that the host walks you to the person. Ask them who they think you should meet.

You leave last-ish to make the most of the people still there. Those are the people most interested in networking because they can't tear themselves away.

Focus on others, not yourself—the leadership precept, of course. A quarter of attenders will be more nervous than you.

They just don't show it and nor should you. See the story of the slimming class trainer in **87**. You could practise this precept:

> Whenever you feel you have difficulties, find someone in a worse position and help them.

If you are feeling nervous, why not enlist some moral support in the form of a business colleague? Inviting a colleague to accompany you will benefit everyone:

○   you will benefit from the extra support

○   your colleague will benefit from the opportunities offered by the event

○   the others at the event will benefit from having a new playmate.

If you can separate from your colleague, even if only towards the end of the event, that will be all to the good. It's rather like taking your feet off the bottom of the pool when you are learning to swim.

One can pathologise all this far too much. 'Just do it' is a useful antidote to that. If you need the advanced form, it is 'Ferchrissakes, just do it!'.

If you have a cultured cast of mind, remember those pesky witches' advice to Macbeth:

> Be bloody, bold, and resolute…
> Be lion-mettled, proud.

103   Remember to create rapport

Yes, rapport is something that can be conjured up from thin air; it isn't just the consequence of meeting that magical 'right' person.

Rapport is the ability to relate to others in a positive and constructive way. Its purpose is to optimise communication, minimise misunderstandings and make it most likely that others will get what we mean (and vice versa, of course). To be honest, it's hard not to create rapport if you follow the precepts in this book: making the other person more important than you, seeking to understand them, showing up and the rest all actively promote rapport.

The best way to build rapport is simply to take a genuine interest in getting to know what's important to the other person. Start to understand them rather than expecting them to understand you first.

13 Improve your tactics

104 Fixing what you talk about

46 suggests not talking about benefits and services, but rather about how your services help your clients to solve problems they have. If you haven't really got a handle on that yet, there's your first task. But, if you think you are doing that well enough, it may be that the people you are talking to really are not interested because your services are just too distant from their needs. This is an occupational hazard of networking. But all is not lost. Shift to talking about how their services help their clients to solve problems. Once there is a sense that both of you have had a crack of the whip, go on, if you have the chance, to the subject of who they know who might have the problems your services help solve, and who you know who might have the problems their services help solve.

To do this, basically you need to have identified who your target markets are (see **50**). You still need to describe to those you encounter how you help people solve their problems, but this explanation has to go with a brief description of the sort of people who have the sort of problems you can help with. I suggest saying that 'these people are in the financial sector', for example, may not be very helpful; better to give concrete examples: accountants, financial advisers or whoever, even (and particularly) if it's not a complete list.

But, overwhelmingly, if you are having difficulties having people understand how your business helps others, it's because you need to improve the stories you tell, or the way you tell them. Do revisit section 8 for a refresher. People won't remember *anything* you say unless you make it memorable. If you don't believe that stories are the best way to do this, you at least owe it to yourself to prove you are right.

I suggest trying it out for a few months and giving it your best shot. For, although people like to have their beliefs about what is right reinforced, they don't like their business failing unnecessarily either.

Story: Eggs (6)

Rex had been going to networking events for some months. He was happy that he was refining the bits and pieces in his portfolio through practice, but he wasn't making much headway in booking meetings. He decided to raise the problem with Julian, a coach who also went to the events.

After going down a number of blind alleys, Julian hit upon the question, 'So what do you talk about, then?'. Rex said he was keen to get over not only that the eggs were high quality (that is only an opinion, after all), by why they were high quality. He covered the breed of hen, the conditions the hens were kept in, the space they had to roam in, the food they were given, the fact that Rex had discovered the hens laid better if they were played the soothing tones of Mantovani and so on. And, Rex went on before Julian could interrupt, how these conditions enhanced both the flavour and the nutritional qualities of the eggs; how, because Rex only delivered locally, the eggs were fresher than those from a wholesaler and so on.

'Whoa!' cried Julian, eventually. 'This is all no doubt fascinating, but how does it help the person you are talking to mention you to their contacts in hospitality? Is it likely that they'll be able to say, "Met this chap Rex. He flogs posh eggs"?'.

As Julian pointed out, Rex would be better to say how his eggs solved problems that his potential clients in the hospitality sector have.

105 Fixing who you talk to

At a networking event, there is a restricted number of people and a restricted period of time in which to reach them. Firstly, if the organisers have produced a list of 'attenders' (actually a list of those who have booked), ask for it if you weren't given it on arrival. If they haven't produced a list—and you've paid an admission fee to the event or a membership fee to the organisation (or both)—complain. It is unprofessional not to provide such a list.

In a room full of strangers, you always need to talk to:

o   the connectors

o   the mavens

o   and the organisers.

(Connectors and mavens are discussed in **27**.) Be there early and work out who these people are and make sure you book one-to-one meetings with all of them. Then who you talk to depends on the purpose of your being there and the outcomes you seek. If you still don't seem to get any traction, whoever you talk to, it's unlikely that who you talk to is the problem.

106 You are not really interested in the people

This could be a tough one. If an event is one of a regular series, the first question to ask is, 'Am I at the right series of events?' If the event attracts people you have little business relation to, it may be better to withdraw and find another event. If that is not possible because there are simply no more suitable events, I suggest remembering the expense incurred in time and money belongs to your business (not you) and it should be spent on furthering the interests of the business. Online networking is always an alternative, however inadequate. I have chosen to ignore this important aspect of networking simply because it is so much harder to do it with any emotional intelligence and there are many good websites that address the behavioural aspects.

However, I suggest a different approach, even if you don't feel it could be possibly appropriate to you (in fact, especially if you feel it isn't appropriate to you).

Ask yourself why you feel you are not really interested in them. Of course, if the cause is temporary—you've lost a certain zest for life following a personal relationship break-up—then really you don't need to bother with this. But, otherwise, once you've answered, 'I just told you, the event attracts people I have little business relation to!', ask yourself this:

> How come it suits me that I go to networking events at which there are no people I have a business relationship with?

And, once you've got rid of the plausible superficial answers—such as that there are no other events—ask the question again. It's worth repeating here that *everyone* is potentially of interest. You just don't know until you extend yourself towards them. They are likely to do the same to you. But, if you give off vibes of lack of interest, you can't blame them for not being interested in you.

Firstly, thinking of the networking event as offering you the chance to help others will help you. Go there with no purpose other than to help others. Now, there's a radical thought! But, you simply cannot predict what will happen as a result.

Secondly, by asking that little question right at the end that so many people either forget to ask (or 'forget' to ask), 'Who do you know who might be interested in what I do?', you open the door to a range of people, none of whom feel the *event* is of value (otherwise they would be there) but whom, precisely because of that commonly shared disconnect with it, might be of interest to you.

If you assume that 75% of those you ask will say no-one, 20% will give you one name and the rest will give you two, you could leave the meeting with half a dozen names. You then contact each one promptly (so that Chris, who gave you the contact, remembers the conversation when you do it) saying, 'I was talking to Chris yesterday [true] and he/she suggested that you might be interested in what I do [true]. Could we arrange to have a conversation about it in the next week or so?' And, don't forget to copy Chris.

It's rude and presumptuous to demand that the person stops what they were doing at the moment you call them just to talk to you for fifteen minutes about something that actually may be of no interest to them (Chris could have got it wrong; the person may not even recall who Chris is).

107 Getting your target market right

This is the target market for your visit to the networking event, not your business's target market, though these could, of course, be the same.

Your target market for the visit must be one about which you can speak cogently, fluently, credibly—and memorably. So, what you say and the market you say it about are inextricably linked. And they also depend on the material you have. It's of little value having interesting material about a market that is not represented at the meeting. It is even worse to talk boringly about the market you actually *are* interested in to someone who is in that market.

108 Getting what you do right

As we saw in **47**, this will be determined by the intentions you set.

It's vital that the listener appreciates what you do. By that, I don't mean that they could sit and pass an examination in what you do—it isn't a lecture—but they should have an idea of how you and your business help clients fix their problems. There seems to me little point in someone being able to repeat that you are an expert in email marketing campaigns if they don't understand what these are or why anyone would want one.

Knowing what you should do next—and then doing it—is the most obvious area where one can improve one's game. Too often—and I am guilty of this myself—one does not follow up a conversation one has had at an event. At the very least you should contact the person and say what a lovely time you had with them. Just:

a thank them for their time

b provide the thing you offered to provide (link to some article on the web, say) c   provide something even if you didn't think to offer it at the time

d   invite them to a follow-up one-to-one, if remotely appropriate (see section 16).

Section 6 has some more tasks you should be keeping up with.

14 You are not doing it right

Introduction

Normally, in a section on sorting out why it's 'not working', one would compile a thorough list of such ways. Then, for each one, one would suggest what to do, think and feel differently or better and more. The list might start:

o   I'm not getting enough/any clients

o   People don't seem to be interested in me

o   I can't get to the nub of what I need to say.

…and go on for some time. In this way the reader would pick their problem, run through the suggested things they could do to make it better; do them; discover that, indeed things do get better, and everyone is happy.

Of course, that little list is not a list of problems: it's a list of symptoms of problems. Unfortunately, when it comes to business networking, there are relatively few symptoms, barely half a dozen really, while the list of practical suggestions is rather long. And, worse, there's no neat correlation between them. It's rather like a tennis student whose problem is a poor return of service. It's a simple thing to be 'not working'. But the number of changes he or she could make to improve their return— some of which would turn out to be constructive and some not relevant on this occasion—are legion (stance, position, anticipatory movements, mental attitude, concentration, focus, first or second serve, tactics for return, choice of racquet, not turning up and so on).

So the approach I take is to focus on the things you could work on. If you do that, it will inevitably mean that at least one of your symptoms—something that's 'not working'—will improve.

'Problems' is perhaps too scary a word: I use it in the sense that, if you keep getting an unwanted outcome (returns of service are out of court), it is worth considering what you should do differently (or better) to stop getting that result. Until it's fixed, it's a problem: this isn't some sort of moral judgement—it's just a problem for the time being.

And, unlike other authors who largely ignore this area—or, if they consider it, only consider it from a behavioural point of view—I claim that the activities need to be addressed in emotionally intelligent ways.

So, first of all, section 3 listed a dozen misconceptions or unhelpful beliefs, any and all of which will shed light on the problems we experience when networking. If fixing them isn't needed, or they don't suit, then there are more specific ideas in this section to deal with problems at networking events. The recommended approach is:

a   be clear as possible in what way it's 'not working' at networking events

b   read through this section identifying all the ideas that ring true

c   put them to one side

d   read through this section again, identifying the issues that could *never* apply to you, and action *them*.

This exercise isn't about reinforcing your beliefs about yourself. It's about overcoming your resistance and getting you into your stretch zone. We are not conscious of most of what's in our minds at any one time. The fact that we honestly believe we do X properly is not sufficient evidence that we do. If the evidence derived from the responses of those around you is that, sometimes, you don't do it properly, you have to accept that as a possibility, however repugnant.

110 However long you think it will take, it will take longer

This is not invariably true, of course, but by and large people are too optimistic in assessing:

o   the time needed to get to know others at networking events

o   the time needed to get into a strong enough relationship with someone they meet that that person will provide them with a strong lead to a prospective client

o   the time needed between that first meeting with a prospective client and pinging the first invoice to them.

So, are you spending enough time on it? Work out how many leads you need, based on the percentage you estimate you can convert into clients, and the value of each client. This will be specific to:

o   the needs of your business

o   the availability of networking forums within travelling distance (you may have to go online to supplement this activity)

o   your willingness to get up early and eat indifferent breakfasts.

Draw up a plan partly to predict your activity per month but, more importantly, so you can record what happened after each event.

Once you have some numbers, I recommend drawing an accurate timeline, placing on it known networking events you are going to attend. Add the follow-up one-to-ones you intend to have with the people you meet at the events. Schedule them a week after the networking event. It's far too early to guess nothing will come from them. So schedule more networking events and repeat.

Remembering that the whole point of networking is to form and develop relationships with people, you may need a 'contact relationship management' (CRM) system to record the information about the people you meet and what was said at the meeting. There are software packages on the market, including free ones, to choose from, though a spreadsheet is good enough. The essential need is to keep tabs on what will become a huge amount of data: if your network is a tree, the CRM data represents the leaves, twigs and branches.

It would be a very good idea to document what you are doing, as you do it, so that in future months you can learn from experience. In particular, what worked and what didn't work. The memory is very fickle and it plays tricks. When you are feeling a tad despondent, it's worth going back and seeing how well you did a few weeks ago.

If your business is in startup, you should aim to have four one-to-one meetings each day you have no fee-earning work. I received this invaluable advice from Darren Shirlaw. I used to set up a day's worth of meetings at Bristol golf club: the person who had the midday slot got to have lunch with me.

This regime requires you to find time to go to the networking events that will reveal the people to invite to the one-to-one meetings. Even if Darren's advice was a counsel of perfection, I doubt that he was anything other than serious. His point is that, if you drag the process out, as a new business, you will run out of startup capital before you have enough income from clients.

There is also the effect of speed. Doing twenty one-to-ones in a month gives you more than doing the same number over six months. You develop a momentum that is positive, if not exhilarating. At the end of each week you can see progress—and that's motivating.

If your business is not in startup and has some clients, you may not need to get so many new clients, but then you don't have so much time to do it in. So, you are not much better off, unless you have devoted your networking activities to creating 'pipelines': relationships with referral partners that deliver you warm leads and referrals without much activity from you.

No business will reach advanced growth while it is still relying on hand-to-mouth leads derived from time-consuming networking. There has to be a better way and it is through business relationships with business people who refer prospects to you. In other words, they help you.

111 There is a threshold of activity you have to reach in order to see results

Do less than this and you might as well not bother to do anything. So, are you working hard enough?

Story: Drugs and alcohol

Nick's business provides advice and guidance to employers with a problem with the use of drugs and alcohol by their staff. This is the sort of problem that few business people will admit to after five minutes of chatting to you at a networking event. Nick had to network with business people who might know businesses with this problem and who might then recommend him to those businesses.

He had to work hard at his networking to reach people who might be embarrassed to be reached in any other way.

How hard you need to work at networking depends on a number of factors:

o how much you need your business to grow by acquiring new clients

o the amount of new business each new client brings

o how willing prospective clients are to open up about their problems

o how good you are at it

o how good, or not, the networking events are that are available to you

o your market sector, and so on.

My view is that, if you do X amount of networking per month and get a certain result, doing twice that amount will deliver more than twice the result. But 'working hard at it' doesn't just mean doing a lot of it. Indeed, doing a lot of it superficially, inauthentically, is probably not worth doing at all, either.

You also need to be intelligent about where you network and who you should talk to when you're there. You need to regularly review progress against targets and periodically change the targets if they turn out to be unrealistic, or modify what you do, or both.

You need to do the right things and do them *well*. And, not just well, but increasingly well. Your performance should become such that others see you as an exemplar within the groups you frequent; a 'go-to' person on the subject of building productive business relationships.

112 You are not doing it properly

This whole book is about giving you chapter and verse on what to do before, during and after. These are tried and tested techniques that have been shown to work the vast majority of times they are tried.

Practice makes perfect. The best analogy is playing a sport or a musical instrument. One just has to practise. The more we practise and the better we practise, the better we get. I suggest that, if you go to ten networking events, one per working day for a fortnight, you will be better at networking events after the tenth one than if you had gone to ten events, one per week. And, you would have attained that level of expertise in two weeks, rather than ten. Those are two strong reasons for seeking out networking events and attending them when you have no fee-earning work to do, or when you can reschedule fee-earning work (which is usually).

Of course, I don't advocate being perfect. Good enough is just fine. If you are good enough, you will be among the most proficient of networkers.

Don't put this book aside. One can easily slip into bad habits and, in particular, it can be easy to forget some of the small detail. Do you remember to ask, at the end of every conversation you have, however short, who else the person knows who *might be* interested in what you do? And, are you practising this to find out how to ask in a way that the other person doesn't find intrusive?

Bad habits can arise from forgetfulness. If I find that, on one occasion, a particular approach was successful—by chance and without my doing anything special—there's a risk of my forgetting it unless I make a point of remembering to do that special thing regularly.

Monitor your progress in a written journal.

Is it all too much? At first, there will be just too much to remember. That doesn't matter. Just do what you remember, linking your experiences back to your management process. Once you have mastered some of the techniques, master some more. None of the techniques is difficult or complicated.

I think the most important things to do first are as follows.

Before you walk through the door:

a   make it about the other person

b   know your purpose in being there

c   know what outcomes you seek

d   set your intentions

e   be early, leave last.

How you are when talking to someone else—you could paraphrase these as 'be interested in the other person':

f   be present

g   listen to the other person

h   ask open questions.

The two most important tasks to carry out at that event are:

i   be prepared to help others, and ask how you can help them

j   find the connectors and mavens and make sure to talk to them.

One reason for suggesting that a networker is not doing it properly is when he or she has their own beliefs about how to do it and won't let go of them, even for five minutes. If those beliefs result in success, stick with them: you are clearly doing it right.

But, if it isn't working, it may be because you are invested in the idea that the ways I am suggesting are, funnily enough, not the best ways of networking and, despite the evidence to the contrary, your ways are better.

That may be true and the issue may be that you are not following your beliefs well enough. But, if you are getting stuck, it is at least worth establishing whether or not the ideas in this book are useful. They aren't guaranteed to work for you, though they probably will; the important thing is that you have to verify whether or not they are useful (I can't evaluate them for you). Unless you give them a reasonable trial, you will never know. So, set an intention to trial them for, say, six months. Only at the end of that period, evaluate whether or not you need to change them to suit your particular circumstances.

But, if you find a better way than something in this book, please tell me!

113 You need to keep in touch

There is nothing so pointless as going to a networking event (which costs time and money), having a productive conversation with someone that really hints that an excellent relationship could be developed and then not contacting them again. Don't wait for them to contact you. On the whole, they won't.

> Story: Follow-up
>
> Rachel specifically asked me to coach her in networking and, even though I say so myself, she became good at it. After six months, we reviewed her progress and I asked her if she had any problems.
>
> 'Not really,' she said. 'Well, only one. Every time I meet someone at a networking event, I have to be the person to follow them up. No-one ever follows me up.'
>
> 'I am afraid that that comes from being a leader,' I said. 'Unfortunately, many people at events do not understand that the idea is to talk to the people you meet there outside the event afterwards. You just have to show them the way. If it's any consolation, remember that, by following up, you develop your business in the way you would like and, more importantly, you are seen to be a leader who knows what she is doing. That can only be a big plus in any networking group.'

Have a system to prompt you to make regular contact with the people you've met. Note that 'regular' doesn't mean frequent. 'Every Christmas' is regular, though I suggest you need to do it more often than once a year. You need to focus on your strongest connections while recognising that attention to some of the others is also important.

You will have to reserve some time for picking up the phone and having a quick chat. It's best to do this when you have something of interest or use to them to say ('I saw on the web the other day that there's been such and such a development in your sector…').

Of course, email (or the social medium of your choice) is ideal for passing on an article or video to someone if you think there's a conceivable chance that it could be relevant to them. People like the idea that someone is thinking about them and, even if you miss, it's the thought that counts.

114 You are not doing enough research

Part of appearing confident at a networking event is knowing that you can reply to pretty much anything anyone says to you; and that you can initiate interesting topics of conversation when next to someone, both of you clutching a so-so glass of wine and a sausage roll.

Researching the attenders before you even arrive is good. If the event is sector-specific or area-specific, mug up on those things. If you aren't remembered after a networking event, why bother to go? People will remember you if:

o   you show an intelligent interest in them and can converse with them on that subject

o   you tell them something interesting, entertaining, thought provoking or just different from what everyone else is talking about.

It's part research and part simple preparation. Make sure you know, as best you can, what the organisers and attenders at the event need.

15 People don't seem to 'rate' you

115 Introduction

There can only be a finite number of reasons why you've assiduously attended networking events yet it isn't working (as well as you had hoped/been told it would). Let's assume that 'it's not working' means you are not receiving enough (or any) leads, referrals or introductions.

Logically, those reasons must be:

a   You are making it up as you go along…

b   …and you are therefore missing many of the tricks that others have learnt. Solution: go back to the beginning of this book and start again, applying what you think could be of value and then apply all the rest of it too. As I said at the start, I don't expect you to believe anything I say (that would, after all, be an expectation on my part), but I say it with sufficient conviction that I believe you will benefit from trying it out.

c   You are doing what this book, or some other book, says but one or more of the following applies:

  ○ you are not doing it often enough

  ○ you are not doing it well enough

    o   you are not doing in the right places, or to/with the right people.

d   You have a variety of beliefs (often called 'limiting beliefs') that are not serving you well.

e   (And this is the interesting one, the one that many people just don't go to.) You are placing obstacles in your own way, but you are not aware of doing so. It is a subconscious process but the fact that you are, by definition, unaware of it doesn't mean it isn't happening. You can't avoid this issue if you want to be successful; and you can't be successful if you don't tackle it.

In the words of the zen saying, this section focusses on:

A person stands in their own shadow and wonders why it is dark.

116 Physical appearance

It has been said that it takes just one tenth of a second for us to judge someone and make a first impression. Even if that were a dramatic exaggeration (and I am not qualified to say) and it took, say, five seconds, that would still be remarkable. Not least because it implies that nothing we say contributes to a first impression that has already been formed before we even open our mouths.

So, while standards of dress have relaxed over the past ten years, it would still benefit people (and I mean men here) to adopt a 'smart casual' style, rather than looking as if they have just been decorating someone's bedroom even if, by the nature of their job, that is what they have just been doing.

Story: Bad breath

Daisy is a tolerant, forgiving soul, but even she had trouble with one person she sat next to at a networking event, so bad was his breath. Often such a problem is within the person's powers to address but, if it is a symptom of a wider problem, best to get it checked by a doctor.

117 You are not letting go of the need to be right

We all need certainties in our lives: beliefs, ideas, feelings about things. The problem comes when we retain our attachment to those certainties even after it is clear they are not serving us anymore. Or, possibly, aren't even certain. Life is never-ending change; the only real certainty is that there are no certainties. Sometimes we hold onto the attachments—because their familiarity makes us feel comfortable—even though the very thing that makes us feel comfortable is the reason we should let go of them.

It helps if business people are right about things. I am not suggesting that business people be wrong about decisions they need to make for the progress of their business. So how would you know when you are being held back by a *need* to be right about some things, perhaps networking, as opposed to just being right?

Firstly, there is a sense of dissatisfaction that things are not right. Things aren't going well. In the story of Damian (see **86**), the absence of clients would have been a big clue, as would the difficulty of finding ever more exotic and implausible reasons for their absence (anything other than the real reason). There is an incongruity between things not happening and one's belief that they should be happening: after all, we are doing everything right, aren't we?

One of the most widely misattributed sayings is:

> *Insanity is repeating the same mistakes and expecting different results.*

Without wishing to diagnose insanity in anyone, it does seem silly to carry on doing something that experience is telling you isn't working. More importantly, it is not in your business's interest to do this. All I suggest is to suspend disbelief, systematically address what you are doing and see if tweaking, or even changing it makes a difference. It is probably worth talking the issue over with someone else (maybe an organiser of the events you go to). It can be very hard to see our blind spots, particularly when we deny we have them.

(We did letting go of being right in **86**.)

118 You come across as needy

Sometimes one meets people at networking events who just give off a sense of neediness. It may be slight but it can become more apparent at repeated meetings. It's possible that the person—let's call them White—isn't at all needy and the other person (Black) is mistaken, or may be projecting their own neediness onto White. But, usually White is needy, and the crucial point is that either:

a   White is unaware of this and is therefore communicating his/her state of mind subconsciously (like we all do, most of the time); or

b   White is aware that he/she can be needy, but is unaware that he/she is communicating it and/or doesn't know how to stop doing so.

Only on rare occasions is White consciously communicating this neediness, and that's because White knows—like we all do—that neediness is unattractive to the point of being off-putting. People metaphorically, or even literally, move away from you if you keep it up, in case they get 'infected' by the neediness.

Neediness is, of course, an expression of the scarcity model: 'I need you to become a client' or 'I need you to give me a lead' because 'I know there isn't enough to go round, and I don't have enough right now'. One of the reasons this is unattractive to other people is that White is essentially putting him/herself in a dependent position, and why would you want someone you hardly know to be dependent on you?

It has to be mentioned that some people would rather be right about a bad situation than go through the risk of changing the situation to a better one (for example, Damian again, in **86**). They as good as create a work situation that conforms to their beliefs around scarcity, so it isn't really surprising that they feel scarcity! But, at least they can be confident that their view of the world is right.

Often, neediness can be crisply diagnosed as running a scarcity model.

Unfortunately, such rational explanations don't always help. The person whose business is really failing, and whose partner is readily pointing this out, needs some serious help to sort it all out. The business person who is using the scarcity model as an excuse ('it must be true since Grandpa told me so') has an easier choice: show up or not.

119 You are 'giving in order to get'

In **32**, I described an accountant who kept a ledger in which he had recorded the value of all the business that had been referred to him so that he could be sure that he didn't refer work of a higher value back.

This true story may be at the very extreme, but it does exemplify a tendency for people to think that a belief that givers gain—which is supposed to mean that one should give unconditionally to others because 'what goes around comes around'—actually means 'I'll give you something but I want something back in return'. This conditional giving by White—which is giving with an expectation of a payback—however subconsciously it is communicated, is experienced by Black as a demand. And people don't like demands being made of them.

Once again, the effect isn't negated because it is experienced subconsciously. I recently encountered a LinkedIn discussion forum in which someone (actually a sales trainer) had initiated a discussion in the usual way, that is, he posted a link to a page on his website. (I don't think this actually counts as initiating a discussion, but let that pass.) The suggestion was that, click on this link and you will be able to read something interesting/ useful/possibly even of value.

On clicking the link, however, a form was displayed requiring me to provide my contact details—name, business name, address and so on. I hadn't got the impression that this was going to be necessary. I felt it had been sprung on me and, worse, it had all the trappings, not just of 'giving something' (the article) 'in order to get something back' (my contact details), but actually of taking my contact details before the article was even forthcoming.

To the extent that the outcome was different from what I had been led to believe it would be, I felt the initial posting was deceptive. It was pretending to be something it clearly wasn't.

It would be remarkable if it weren't so commonplace that a business person is impelled by his/her scarcity model to initiate a business relationship in such a way that it guarantees the failure of that relationship. After all, who wants a business relationship with someone who misleads you?

120 You come across as inauthentic

Story: Barman (52 coins)

I used to work with Desmond in a London pub where we were barmen. He was among the better staff: quick, efficient, he'd always give the right change, and he was always affable and friendly. The trouble was that he had a little habit of saying, when asking for the money, 'That'll be 52 coins of the realm, please'. (Yes, it was that long ago.) The very first time one heard this, it might have raised a slight smile; after ten or more times in one evening it was getting wearing and, after three months, it was homicide-inducing.

It was the clear inauthenticity of the way Desmond related to the customers that grated. It encouraged one to find further 'faults' and soon anything in his manner, however normal, became suspect. One rapidly came to the conclusion that, rather than being a barman, he was someone playing the role of a barman. But it was the way that he drew attention to it that was so fascinating; no-one could mistake the performance for what it was.

(Over time, I actually came to the conclusion that he was someone playing the role of an actor badly playing the role of a barman. After all, many actors have been bar staff out of necessity; they could convincingly play a bar person at the drop of a hat.)

I never discovered whether Desmond understood what he was doing or the effect it had on others. But, in truth, whether as a bar person or a networker, inauthenticity jars on other people. It is one thing people are very sensitive to and it never convinces.

Whether you are suggesting that you are more successful than you are, or that your business is larger than it is ('Henry

Bloggins Intergalactic—consultancy for the cosmos. Closed Wednesday afternoons'), or that your clients have been more prestigious than they are, or that your services are more exotic than they are, you will be found out. (I have never understood why someone, calling themselves an 'international coach' because they have a client in Paris to whom they talk on Skype, thinks that the location of the client is an indication of their prowess as a coach. But what do I know?)

Of course, people you talk to won't actually reveal to you the niggling doubt (or even irritation) they have. You end up wondering, like Karen, why, however much networking you do, you don't get much success.

People are tempted to be inauthentic for two sets of reasons:

a   They think other people will be impressed. Actually, the people probably would be impressed—if they believed it. But, as my mother used to say, it's not what you say, it's the way that you say it that counts.

b   They fear that other people will think that the person they believe they really are, and the business they think they have, will not be interesting or compelling to others. This is about their sense of worth and has nothing to do with how others perceive their business.

Someone who started their business the day before the networking event they are now at has every reason to trumpet the fact (and get as much sympathy and encouragement as possible from all concerned while it lasts).

Someone who is nursing a set of negative beliefs around their own value is skating on thin ice: the reasonable question to ask is, if they have an inaccurate idea of their business and the services it provides, how objective would their view of my business, its services and needs be? This is not a promising start on which to attempt to build a business relationship.

The British like to affect a self-deprecating modesty that can verge on the inauthentic and annoying ('Yes, it's true that I did rescue the Queen singlehandedly from a towering inferno, while suffering from a slight cold, but I don't like to talk about it').

I'm suggesting that the characteristics we should want to convey at a networking event are our integrity, our credibility as providers of goods and services and our conviction in ourselves and our goods and services. None of this, nor anything else positive and beneficial, can be communicated if we are actually pretending to be someone we are not. People will pick up on one bit of insincerity and apply it to all you say.

Don't underestimate the extent to which anyone's thoughts, beliefs and intentions are picked up subliminally by those they speak to. If someone is pretending to be what they are not, it will be picked up. (Apparently, people start to be able to detect this incongruity from the age of eighteen months. So just don't network with toddlers.)

121 You are not 'showing up'

As Woody Allen is said to have said:

> 80 percent of success is showing up.

For me, showing up is literally being at the events.

In particular turning up to an event you've booked and probably paid for, but which suddenly seems less enticing than before. Many people who are running a scarcity model may well decide that, if an opportunity to discuss a possible prospective client shows up, that is worth taking up instead. Well, it is worth doing, but will it really vanish in a puff of smoke if you reply to the invitation, 'Sorry, I have a prior engagement, could we make it two hours later?' And then, if your contact happens to be stopping over at Heathrow for two hours waiting for a connecting flight to New York, you probably do have a good reason to duck the networking event. But, if they are on the industrial estate down the road, I doubt they will mind waiting, or bringing the meeting forward.

Personally, I would do this even when requested to do billable work. Any client of mine is a business; the people in it have to juggle their diaries. Unless it is impossible for the date to be changed (and, of course, I do ask—maybe they want me to sit in on a meeting with one of their clients who is on a stopover in Heathrow), I will ask if it would be convenient to do it some other day (usually the next or previous day). Those with a scarcity model have such a fear that the client will sack them and not pay their invoices if they don't agree to show up to the client's site when demanded that they don't show up to the networking event.

A belief that recognises that being at a networking event isn't, or shouldn't be, a wholly selfish act (and that actually the others there will miss you) should help, too.

Be present mentally when you're there. Keep focussed on the event in hand and, in particular, the person to whom you are talking. Some people give the impression their mind is elsewhere. If their mother is ill in hospital, that's wholly understandable. But sometimes I get the impression that people don't apply themselves to the networking event with the same degree of professionalism that they would apply to a meeting with a prospect, or when doing fee-earning work.

That's surprising, because one of the things everyone does at the event is to size each other up. Betray a lack of professionalism at the event and the others will have no choice but to assume that it reflects a lack of professionalism in your work. And, if they do that, they will be markedly less keen to mention you to any of their contacts when the time comes.

And it's not just professionalism: it relates to commitment, willingness to participate and so on. If you are not committed to the event, you may need to think (a) what others there infer about you, and (b) how that has come about. As a temporary solution, 'acting as if' will work, providing you don't overdo it and it becomes false.

The positive side is that, by making a good showing, you can increase your standing in the group simply by the way you present yourself. Simply by showing up.

122 You come across as a dependent person

To be honest, I suspect that some independent people don't go networking because they have little intention of helping others, and little belief others will help them. The story *Ledger* (**32**) shows such a person. But they may well send a colleague or a junior, so there is still a chance to make contact with their business.

It is when someone dependent shows up at a networking event that we have a problem. Their expectation that they will be 'fed' by the others there can be difficult to separate from neediness. In fact, it often is neediness.

Luckily, the antidote to dependency is easy to describe and usually easy to put into action, unless the person is determined to be like that. Essentially, they should replace a need to be helped by others with a willingness to help others. As one person put it,

> Look for someone in a worse situation than you are in, and go and help them.

If it is difficult to make such a big switch, then:

○ tell yourself you will try it for one event, or one day, or one week, month, whatever you feel you can manage

○ be curious about what will happen

○ assure yourself you will switch back if you need to, provided you have given this approach a fair shot.

123 You feel pushed outside your comfort zone

If you feel you are outside your comfort zone, ask, metaphorically speaking, how large your comfort zone is and how far outside it you feel. As **29** suggests, what's outside your comfort zone is not unmitigated stress: it's a 'stretch zone'. An area where you can stretch yourself. The adrenaline may be running, but that's good: you will perform better.

A perfect example in the world of networking is the presentation. Many organisers of networking events like to add the attraction of a speaker. The speaker duly stands up and gives five tips for using LinkedIn, or whatever. Half the audience is thinking, 'I couldn't do that', 'I'm not going to do that', 'If wild horses on their bended knees begged me to say five words to the group, I would refuse'.

The problem here is that, although they are comfortable listening to the presentation, even the idea of being asked to give it pushes them to the edge of their comfort zone and just a few more inches puts them into stress.

Given that networking events do not offer the chance to make 'keynote' speeches to 500 people for an hour, any opportunity to do a presentation should be grabbed. Firstly, it raises your profile and your credibility considerably. Secondly, it widens your comfort zone hugely: if you can do that, you can do anything else you need to do at a networking event. Thirdly, you will probably be giving out information and insights that at least some in the audience find helpful.

Just respect your audience and practise doing it well. If you are part of a networking club with many branches, offer to do a tour of all the branches doing the same presentation. You will be good at it by the end of that process and you will have learnt a lot that you can apply to any other presentation you are asked to do. Apart from anything else, organisers are often in need of good speakers, and I recommend being known to be a *good* speaker, not just as *a* speaker.

Some events allow members to talk for two minutes to the people on their table. So use that as a starting point. Most presentations to the whole group are no more than twenty minutes and, if that's too long, suggest to a fellow networker that you pair up and do two ten minute slots on related subjects.

Encourage and embrace challenges to move into your stretch zone. Two things are certain:

o   if you stay in your comfort zone, the comfort zone will shrink without you noticing it (this, sadly, happens to many older people)

o   consciously being in your stretch zone will widen your comfort zone: what you thought was a stretch becomes comfortable.

124   You have 'fears'

The blanket prescription for *fear of the event* is, 'Feel the anxiety and do it anyway'.

As I've said elsewhere (**87**):

a   it isn't fear (an instinct), it's anxiety (or worry)

b   half the people in the room have it, too

c   it's natural and even to be welcomed in moderation (it's adrenaline)

d   it's overcome by confidence, and confidence comes from

   o   knowing what you are doing, so do your research

   o   practising, so keep doing it (however terrible you think the first times were)

e   follow the guidance in this book

f   enlist help from the organiser

g   and be early.

Story: Feeling a fraud

Bruce's company was stuck. It had actually been stuck for ten years, so it seemed likely that Bruce was quite good at keeping it in that stuck position. Rather like landing a helicopter on a ship rolling in a gale (so I am told), it is hard to stop either the business or the copter crashing.

After some substantial conversations, Bruce blurted out, 'I'm scared that, if we become well known, we will be discovered by the media and exposed as frauds'. Well, I didn't expect that one. Bruce didn't think his company was a fraud, it was just the fear that it would be unjustly accused of being one that haunted him. Why he thought he might be exposed, he couldn't say.

I mention this story lest anyone feel that *fear of success* is absurd: who doesn't want to be successful? Lots of people. In fact, almost everyone who isn't running a fear of failure is running a fear of success.

Both these fears paralyse the business person: 'If I do X, something good/bad will happen, sooner or later (probably sooner). It will be a failure… It won't work. I'll be ridiculed… etc, etc.' It's one of the reasons they do poorly at networking events, or don't even show up at all.

We use these fears as reasons not to move forward, to take the next step. (It's not just, 'If I try to move forward, something bad will happen'. It's, 'Whatever I do, it will end in failure'.) However, what we are refusing to step towards is the opportunity to be interdependent, to form prosperous business partnerships with others and to see our business bloom.

125 You are doing avoidance activity

Avoidance activity is something you do rather than walk into a crowded room full of people you don't know who are all talking to each other. It's understandable. But in the words of a shoe manufacturer, 'Just get on with it'.

You have really got to decide which is the more important thing. If 'avoidance activity' is actually paid work for a client that cannot be done on any other day, it isn't avoidance activity, it's a clash in the diary. But, if it is doing paid work that could be done the next day because, frankly, the client doesn't care when it's done and you decided it was going to be done that day in the first place, then it's avoidance activity.

Once again, it's worth reminding yourself that you are supposed to be doing this networking for your business's sake, not yours.

A subset of this approach is the 'my business isn't ready for me to start this' line. Rubbish. Go to an event and tell everyone that your business isn't fully set up but it will be 'awesome', 'incredible' or even 'I have quiet hopes for its success'— whatever floats your boat. It's never too early to talk about it.

Unfortunately, networking provides you with opportunities that can't be obtained in other ways, at least not in a two hour period. Only you can say whether your business really needs you to be at a networking event but, if you are not sure, then it does.

Networking injects novelty into your day-to-day work. Sometimes, to be sure, not much novelty. But you won't know how much, and how novel, unless you submit to the experience. So deal with this as an apparently unwanted shove outside your comfort zone. It's not that the substitute activity isn't worth doing. It's that it isn't worth doing that day as much as going to a networking event is worth doing.

126 You procrastinate

Serious procrastinators procrastinate whatever the context. It's as if the adult, grown-up, rational, professional part of their brain just knows that they should be following up those people they met at the networking event but somehow that's just not as interesting as doing the crossword, or watching that amusing cat video. The adult gets hijacked by the child who just wants to play and the adult can't or won't step in and lay down the law.

Sometimes, when we avoid doing something, it's because we fear the failure that might come from not doing it well. So, we fail to suggest a follow-up meeting to someone at a networking event because we fear they will say no. Or, we fear they will say yes, and we'll do it badly.

We believe that knowing that someone doesn't want to meet us is worse than not knowing either way; so we avoid finding out. But so what? Let go of your need that they meet you. Or that they like you. This is about kissing frogs, as Sarah Owen assures me. You have to kiss a lot of them in this game and, if you do, you won't mind the ones that stubbornly refuse to metamorphose into frog princes and frog princesses because there are enough who do that it doesn't matter.

I suggest this rule: follow up every person you meet within two days of meeting them. If you don't do it within two days, don't bother to do it at all because they will be so offended you took so long, they won't want to talk to you. And if you don't get to meet them, what was the point of going to the event?

It's not so terrible to have a few rules governing your work if they make you more effective and efficient.

(And, I am happy to say, there are tasks that you can not only procrastinate about but which you should cross off your 'to do' list altogether. Cold calling being top of that list.)

Procrastination is not being lazy. Procrastination is a failure to prioritise; whereas laziness is just indolence. Indolence is an unwillingness to do anything rather than lose the pleasure of doing nothing. Believe me, I know!

127 'Good enough' versus perfectionism

The phrase 'good enough' was brought into prominence by the paediatric psychiatrist DW Winnicott. He was talking about the development of small babies and emphasising the role the mother (or the primary care giver in her absence) has in their development.

Though much of this big subject is irrelevant to business networking, there is a key relevant point. Winnicott emphasised that the mother need only be 'good enough'. The mother does not need to be perfect. Babies have developed over millennia by natural selection to be able to survive despite the activities of their parents.

When I encounter resistance to this phrase (which is surprisingly often) it is usually, I feel, because people misunderstand it. It's almost as if they think it means 'not good enough', not acceptable, not as good as it could be, not as good as I could do it. But note that the phrase 'good enough' contains the word 'good'. It doesn't contain the word 'rubbish'.

In some professions or situations, 'good enough' has to be pretty close to perfection. For example, a good enough operation by a brain surgeon is going to have to be damn good in order to minimise the risk of disaster.

But in, say, networking? The idea of a *perfect* marketing campaign is ridiculous. There would be disagreement over what constituted 'perfect' and over how to measure it, before everyone realised you can't measure it anyway. But it's also not necessary. A 'good enough' networking operation is one that brings in enough good enough clients at a good enough rate and in good enough time.

I'm very happy with the graphic design and the web development that was done for me. They're good. Good enough for my needs. Anything more would have been prohibitively expensive to no real benefit to my business.

Perfection is a way the mind has of stopping us moving forward. 'I can't take the next step because I haven't done this one perfectly yet'. Of course, one never will do it perfectly; one can always find a flaw, and that's the point.

Many people in business, however, feel they have to deliver perfect service—and then beat themselves up when it's pointed out that they aren't doing this. I have to say that, in some cases, the opportunity to beat themselves up is the purpose of the whole exercise, however sad that is.

Failing to recognise that their approach to networking is good enough can be a problem for networkers. Business people are often confident that they know what they are doing in delivering products or a service—they know what the steps are in the process and they understand how to do them—but that clarity clouds over when it comes to the processes of networking. The key thing is that networking, by being about relationships between people, ends up in the domain of emotional intelligence. And emotional intelligence suggests that 'good enough' is when it is delivering good enough results.

128 How much trust is there?

Story: Lack of trust

I was once asked to work with a business that, outwardly, seemed to be doing well. For some reason I forget, the board wanted me to interview each member of the business—either individually or in small groups. As a result of that, it was possible to draw up a picture of how the board members were viewed by the rest of the business.

One finding was very prominent: the staff believed that the directors didn't trust them.

To say that the board members were surprised by this is an understatement. It was almost as if the sheer concept was completely beyond their minds to comprehend. As it happened, I was talking to Rona, one of the directors, a session or two after delivering this unwelcome news. The survey had shown that the staff were pretty hacked off by the extent to which she micromanaged them. They didn't like it and it achieved nothing. Had she let go of her need to micromanage them, we agreed, it was likely the staff would become more motivated, and therefore would do a better job.

So, I asked her why she did it. Quick as a flash, she replied, 'Because I don't trust them'. She then spent twenty minutes trying to deny she'd said that. Unfortunately for her, we were not the only people in the room.

Why would anyone micromanage their team if they thought the team didn't need it? And why would the boss have to look over their work every five minutes? Because Rona didn't believe they would do it properly unless she scrutinised them to this degree. This was just lack of trust. It wasn't a rational assessment of the capabilities of these people. Interestingly, although Rona wouldn't let me go very far with this, we did get as far as my pointing out that it was unlikely every person who worked for her was actually untrustworthy (not least because she had recruited each of them). And, further, I suggested, when people have a blanket mistrust of other people, without cause, it is worth considering that, actually, they don't trust themselves.

At this point, Rona smiled in a way that told me the penny had dropped.

We often see in others, and judge in them, what we judge in ourselves. Often, the perceived failing we judge in ourselves— in Rona's case, she didn't trust herself—gets projected unconsciously onto others.

Trust and the lack of it is an important issue in networking. Amy is unlikely to refer one of her clients to me, however much she is convinced I can help them, if she doesn't trust me (more in **41**). And, like Rona's staff, there is little realistically that I can do to 'prove' my trustworthiness to her. I'm not even sure that 'trustworthiness' is a useful concept: isn't it just reliability and predictability, as in 'trust her to get it right'? The issue is with Amy and it is unlikely to have started recently. If I meet Amy at a networking event then, from a business perspective, it is probably best if we keep our exchanges to pleasantries about the weather and the price of fish.

But, if it is me who isn't trusting of others, then it is worth my thinking how the above applies to me.

How to trust others? You may have had some unfortunate experiences in life, trusting people who have then let you down. However damaging that was, it is in the past. Just because someone, years ago, behaved in an untrustworthy way does not mean the next person you meet will be untrustworthy.

I suggest an evidence-based approach. Assume—until, or if, you have evidence—that you *can* trust someone. A difficulty in doing this may be linked with your approach to stretching yourself.

One nasty little human foible is that, if you treat someone as if you don't trust them (or you think they are stupid, or incompetent), they will tend towards fulfilling that perceived belief. If you keep showing someone how to do something because you think they're incompetent, in the end, they will just keep waiting for you to show them each time.

So, behave towards someone as if you do trust them, and they are likely to reward you.

129 How committed are you?

A quick rummage around the internet reveals that many people consider a commitment to be little more than a promise, or an intention, or a willingness to do, or not do, something.

I don't think this hits the nail on the head. Surely a commitment to something is more than a willingness? It includes the belief that the willingness is well placed, that it is worth doing the thing. And this doesn't have to be something you believe in—it could be something that a partner believes in and your commitment to it is determined by your commitment to them. It includes an intention to continue doing it in the face of adversity.

It is in this more complex sense that I talk about commitment in this book. Commitment is an essential component of partnership, in other words of productive business relationships. It is a way out of power struggle and dead zone (see also **40**).

If your networking activity isn't working, a question to ask could be, 'How committed am I to it working?' 'What reservations do I have about it that haven't come to the surface?'. If you draw a blank, ask someone else to ask you these questions and have them do their best to coach the answers from you. A good start is to ask, 'If I were to know what the reservations are that haven't come to the surface yet, they would be…'.

Go back to the basic networking event. You don't feel like going. You may well have some plausible reasons why you needn't go on this occasion (it's raining). But, are these really just covers? How committed are you to it? Don't you realise that your absence will be a disappointment to others who do make the effort?

130 Are you assertive?

Being assertive means respecting yourself and other people; seeing people as equal to you, not better than you or less important than you. And, it is achieved through open, direct and honest communication.

Assertiveness is essential when networking, both at networking events and in one-to-one meetings. Saying what you mean is essential particularly, as we saw in **87**, because we cannot be sure that the other person got the message quite right.

Some people describe a continuum from passive to aggressive behaviour with assertiveness somewhere in the middle. A sort of punching someone in the face, but not too hard. Just assertively.

This can't be right. Assertiveness is completely different from aggression. When there is aggression, we are either in, or want to be in, a fight. If the aggression is physical, it is violence. (Let's hope a networking event doesn't come to that!) But withdrawal from another person, if it has the energy of a fight, can still be experienced as passive aggression. For example, ignoring someone who wants to speak to you at a networking event is passive aggression (and that *does* happen!).

When we are being assertive we are able to speak up and give our opinions, or ask for what we want in a way that does not result in the other person getting defensive (because there is no fight). In a nutshell, assertiveness is saying clearly what you would like to have happen.

Story: Assertiveness course

Jane went on an assertiveness course. We asked how it went, and she said it was OK, but she still couldn't make people do what she wanted.

This is a true story, and it reminds me of the joke about the trainer who was asked how his assertiveness course was being received. 'It must be good', he replied, 'no-one has complained about it'.

I don't believe that people fail to be assertive because they don't know how (although that may be true as well). They aren't assertive because they believe:

o they do not have the right to be assertive

o they don't really know what it is they want to assert

o or, possibly, that something bad will happen if they are assertive.

So, to cut through this particular behaviour, try new behaviours that are likely to give you new experiences. These will help change your feelings and beliefs about the subject and reinforce the new behaviour.

The top three things to do are:

a *Plan in advance what you are going to say*
Visualise what you are going to say. Imagine yourself being positive. Rehearse the words if you need to.

b *Use the right words*
'I would like X to happen so that Y results' ('I'd like to have a follow-up one-to-one meeting so that we can see if there is any benefit in working together').

c *Act 'as if'*
We are all influenced in some way by other people's behaviour. If they look and sound convincing, we are more likely to be influenced by them.

  o Look the part: use positive body language to reinforce your messages.

  o Sound the part: underline your messages with the appropriate tone.

  o Avoid words that weaken the power of your messages, for example, *could, sorry, not usually, maybe, I don't suppose…, may, might, possible, perhaps, er…, um…*

131 How motivated are you?

Motivation comes from within. Trying to motivate someone else is usually a hit and miss affair. Equally, expecting someone else to motivate you is asking too much of them. That said, most people who run networking events for profit (as opposed to events organised by chambers of commerce, law firms and accountants) do think they are in the business of motivating their members. This is a more helpful approach than any other, so let's not knock it. But what they should be aiming to do is create a positive context, a facilitating environment, in which the networkers motivate themselves. The reason is clear: motivated members of the group are likely to be more successful in their networking, and the organiser can bask in that success, not entirely unreasonably.

So, how to motivate oneself?

a   Even if others can't *make* you be motivated, they can help you to be. So associate with people, including the organisers of networking events, who can help you in this way.

b   Show to yourself, before you start, that what you propose to do is achievable. If your expectations are unrealistic, let go of them. On the other hand, if you just think of yourself as a free spirit, flitting from canapé to canapé, you will probably be disappointed too. Make a plan; give yourself achievable targets and review your progress.

c   Practise some self-development. Use this book and other resources to learn to be better at networking. Remember that we learn when we are in our feelings, so make sure you have good experiences when you practise new techniques, even if they only arise from a constructive and positive review of what went wrong.

d   Discuss your success with friends, family and business colleagues (you may have to be careful whom you choose here; you want the positive ones, not the complaining ones). Talk through with trusted people where you could do better.

e   If funds permit, hire a business coach or mentor (one who understands and works with EI).

IV What comes next?

16 One-to-one meetings

132   One-to-ones are the heart of building a network

Networking events are not the place to develop networking relationships. (They are where you start them.) The situation is often not conducive to good conversation. More importantly, by definition, I hope I have shown that networking events provide the chance to meet lots of people whom you are unlikely to bump into in any other way. Why deprive yourself of the chance to begin to get to know some of them and, indeed, why deprive others of the chance to start to get to know you?

Networking events should best be considered as 'beauty contests' in which you determine who you are going to invite to a one-to-one meeting. Who those people are depends on what your purpose in networking is and on the wider purpose of your business. Think of the follow-up one-to-one as a forum for acquiring, developing and nurturing more business relationships.

Depending on the stage of your business and its needs, follow-up meetings could be for research, to practise your presentation skills to captive audiences of one (I hold my hand up to that one) or for many other reasons.

However, on the majority of occasions, we have follow-up one-to-one meetings with people we meet at networking events because there is a possibility that they may know prospective clients, they may know people who may know prospective clients or they may put other work our way. And they talk to us for precisely the same reasons. Of course, it's possible that they will become a client too, though whether they embark on a one-to-one with you with that outcome in mind is unlikely (they don't know enough about you and they know you don't know enough about them).

I believe that the best business relationships are those in which each partner provides a stream of referrals to the other. The stream may only be a trickle—one a quarter, perhaps. That may be all the other party needs. However, the vast majority of business relationships are not so rich (no referrals are forthcoming). They don't need to be and, indeed, no-one could cope if they were. Desirable and profitable relationships come in many flavours and I stick to this in this book.

> Story: New recruits (1)
>
> Nathan runs a mature business offering very specific training for business people. Although he could do the marketing and selling himself, he is not a marketer nor a seller and believes (possibly correctly) that he isn't so good at these tasks.
>
> What he needs is someone, or some people, who already know businesses who recruit graduates. Of course, other training companies make up one such group, but probably not a fertile one for Nathan. Nathan duly attended networking events, talking to others about his new venture. Everyone agreed it was a great idea and certainly something that was needed, though none of them said it was of use to their business (and, in many cases, it wouldn't have been).
>
> At one event Nathan bumped into just the sort of person he was looking for. Eleanor works in a recruitment agency. They both quickly clicked and Eleanor readily agreed to Nathan's suggestion of a follow-up one-to-one.

133 How to invite someone to a one-to-one

It's important at this stage not to start having expectations of the other person, or to make demands on them (however subconsciously), or even to imagine what a networking relationship with them would be like.

As having a chat with someone you meet at an event afterwards is a perfectly respectable step to take, I would invite someone to a one-to-one via email, roughly as follows:

o 'I enjoyed our conversation. I would be interested/fascinated/intrigued to find out more about your business and maybe to tell you a little more about mine. Perhaps we could meet at your office/a local café/etc.'

Don't mention any expectations you might have of the meeting or any future relationship (after all, at this stage you don't have any!). The purpose of this meeting is to find out more about the other person's business and let them find out more about yours. The outcome will be your decision as to whether you want to pursue the relationship.

134 Structure of a follow-up one-to-one meeting

As with everything else, before you have a follow-up one-to-one, you need to know what your purpose in having the meeting is going to be and what outcomes you seek from it. I suggest that one useful purpose is to establish whether the other person is one you can help. (You may as well start as you mean to go on.)

A follow-up one-to-one needn't have any structure. But, of course, less time and resources will be wasted if there is some sort of a structure. Always be willing to discuss the structure with the other person!

Plan for the conversation to be no more than an hour, with each side having roughly 25 minutes to talk about their business, themselves and how the other person can help them. This allows for pleasantries and the purchase of drinks from the bar.

Be sure to use section 10 as an essential part not just of your preparation, but also your handling of the meeting.

I know you've already met, so you ought to know who each other is, but it is important for each party to say what their purpose is in having the conversation, and what outcomes they would like to seek from the meeting. This is not the time to be coy. The other person may not have thought about this, so you will have to ask them something like, 'What do you expect to get out of this meeting?'. If you want to come across as a seasoned player, ask if there is anything you should talk about that isn't relevant to this meeting but which could be discussed another time.

One party takes centre stage and talks to the other about their business, themselves and anything relevant to any potential relationship. If at all possible, get the other party to do this first. This will mean that, when it's your turn, you can talk to whatever they said in their briefing.

There's actually quite a lot you can usefully find out about the other person. It needs to be done in a light way, but it is important not just to let the conversation ramble as it might if you had no purpose. Adopt a coaching approach here when it's their turn to speak, asking them open questions to ensure you learn as much as you can. Even though you may have explained this structure in the invitation, don't bank on the other person having prepared. You need to prepare beforehand so you can coach them in talking well. (Of course, after you have done a few of these, it will all come naturally.)

Here are some topics each of you needs to find out about the other person:

○ The business:

- What does it do? Products and services.

- What is the purpose of the business; what outcomes have been set for it?

- How you can help their business and vice versa: contacts, introductions, information and so on. Ask them directly, 'How can I help you?' Tell them directly the help you need.

- Who do they know through their business, or outside it, who might be useful to you (not just prospective clients, but people who know prospects)? Likewise, who do you know who could be of use to them?

- Who do you and they know through your businesses, or outside them, who might be useful?

○ You also need to find out more about each other as human beings:

- Personal aspirations at work, outside work?

- What do you each like, dislike?

- What have each of you achieved; what are your interests outside work?

(As an aside, people's interests outside work are often interesting. My, until then, separate interests of music and writing led me to a job as a music critic and feature writer on *Fanfare*—the prestigious US classical music magazine—through a networking contact.)

If you feel that a one-to-one didn't go as well as you imagined it would, start with sections 11 to 15 to diagnose how you can do it better next time.

135   Show and tell

In the bit, 'What does your business do?', some professions have a great opportunity to be really compelling here. Coaches, mentors, advisers and so on should offer some free coaching, mentoring, advising at a one-to-one meeting. And be completely open about this ('I find that the best way for someone to grasp what I do is to experience a bit of it').

These people can often tell seriously useful stories containing general tips and ideas. I find there is no limit to the amount of coaching/mentoring/training/etc that a business will benefit from. So, giving some away beforehand doesn't affect how much I could subsequently provide as paid work. It will, at the very least, enable the other person to get a really good idea of what I do. Personally, I offer to present some of the models I use (for example, the behaviour cycle, 31). This usually turns into a coaching session. I include this as part of the invitation to a one-to-one ('It would be good to find out more about what you do and perhaps I may show you one or two of the models I use?').

If you don't have any models, do consider whether you could have. Models are valuable because they are repeatable, highly communicative and, above all, visual. People can grasp a lot of information in a diagram that it would be tedious and time consuming to enumerate.

Whatever sort of professional you are, it is usually possible to relate what you do to whatever the other person does. It is essential that a 'show and tell' is not perceived to be about you, but about the things you do, and their effects on your clients, that the other person will find interesting/useful/amusing. You have to be careful that the other person does not feel you are offering to help them find out where their business has gone wrong in an ill-disguised attempt to sign them up as a client.

What you don't do, I humbly suggest, is say, 'Would you like a free thirty minute meeting so we can discuss what I do?' Or even worse—and I have heard this—'...and we can discuss how I might help you'. This is all scarcity model stuff. It's off-putting and is, therefore, counterproductive. It's pushy. Being attractive is such a better way of doing it. But some people feel they have to say it.

Firstly, 'Would you like a free thirty minute meeting' is a sales pitch (even if you don't think it is, the other person will, so it is). Secondly, the word 'free' is absurd: you should have no intention of charging for this meeting and the other person should have no intention of paying you for it. Thirdly, 'thirty' is also ridiculous: you're hardly going to stop the clock at thirty minutes and demand the other person get their chequebook out if they expect you to finish the sentence.

Someone may not have the chutzpah to say to someone's face, 'Would you like a free thirty minute meeting...', but they'll write it in an email invitation to a one-to-one afterwards.

If I were a financial adviser, I might (tentatively) say, 'May I suggest something?' The suggestion ought to be relevant to what the other person has said but, provided you believe it is, it doesn't matter if it isn't: the other person recognises that they haven't had a full consultation with you, and appreciates the thought. However, any taint of selling has to be absent from the offer.

Much of the above applies to who you know, too. Of course, you have to be reasonably certain that the person you know and whose name you are just about to give to a complete stranger is going to be happy about this. Usually they are, because people are like that. People like to help other people, on the whole, and one of the tragedies of so many business people, particularly men, is that they are so unwilling or unable to ask for help.

136 The most important thing to ask

The most important thing to ask, at the end of a one-to-one, is:

Who do you know who might be interested in this?

Not, 'Do you know anyone who is interested in this?'

If you ask the latter, it immediately prompts the automatic, let's-get-this-over-with-as-quickly-as-possible response: 'No'. On the other hand, 'Who do you know...' presupposes the person knows someone and, as you are only asking whom they know who may be—or may not be—interested, it is hard for someone to say they don't know *anyone* like that.

137 How to decide what happens next

As the conversation continues, you are likely to be forming an opinion about what you want to happen next. Your intuition will tell you. There is a wide range of options, not all mutually exclusive: one of you might decide to discuss becoming the client of the other; you may want to keep in touch because the other person is an interesting source of information; you may even click on a personal level and develop a friendship.

Most likely, you will agree to keep in touch (that means outside networking events) and see what happens. If you feel you might want to mention the other person to people you meet in the future, you owe it to those people in the future to find out more about the other person so that you have a good idea why you'd mention him or her to them.

The best thing, of course, if there seems to be some benefit to doing it, is to have a second, and perhaps even a third, one-to-one so that you really get to know each other.

Story: New recruits (2)

It goes without saying that Nathan and Eleanor hit it off straight away. Eleanor was more than happy to follow Nathan's idea for the structure of the meeting, which ran on for well over two hours. They anticipated some of the following stages—but only in part. It was then necessary for Nathan to plan carefully what he would propose at the next meeting, so that it wasn't repetitive but did address some points omitted from the first one.

For most people, most of the time, it works well but, as Nathan found out, one always has to be prepared to improvise.

17 Conclusion

138 Conclusion

Ultimately, there are only three things to bear in mind for successful networking:

a   Businesses are just the relationships between people. The totality of the relationships between the people in the business and between them and those outside it. This means networking relationships are included; they're part of the business. They are more important than most people give them credit for. This means these relationships need to be given more time and effort than most people give them if there is to be any point in going to networking events.

b   Approach networking with the right attitude. 'Givers gain' is not a platitude. It represents a truth about reciprocity in all relationships. Approach running a business (of which going to networking events is a key aspect) with a giving attitude. It will always deliver gains that a parsimonious approach cannot. 'Make the other person more important than you' is the single most useful precept to apply.

c   Showing up—literally and metaphorically—is essential. If you are not there, no-one will know who you are. Make 'to be remembered' an intention for every networking event.

After all, if they forget you five minutes after you've left the building…

Happy networking.

139 In the end

Story: Maggie (2)

Some months later, I had a call from Maggie. She reported she'd joined a business networking group, had been attending regularly and was now helping to organise it. She'd been to a business fair at which there was a speed networking event (the sort of event that is designed to create maximum stress for the minimum return). She enthusiastically told me she had made a special point of attending it to find out what it was like.

Much more recently, I contacted her to see if she was happy to appear in this book. She said, 'I'm very happy for you to mention that story. It's not a story I'm embarrassed about and it has helped shape me as a person and business owner for the better.'

Appendix 1: Principles of networking

The principles of networking are principles only insofar as they are beliefs that many networkers have found consistently useful. By and large, they state what is going on, whereas the precepts (appendix 2) state what a networker should do.

As with everything else in the book, approach them with curiosity. Practise following them to see if they are true for you.

They are summarised here. More can be found at the references provided.

Numbers in bold refer to topics, not pages.

Going to a networking event isn't networking   **7**
Networking is the creation and nurturing of work relationships with other business people. Networking events are not set up to facilitate this and you have to have separate one-to-one meetings with people for this purpose. Networking events allow you to choose with whom you are going to have one-to-one meetings.

Givers gain: networking provides a forum for reciprocity   **28**
People who are generous, and are seen to be generous, attract people who want to be generous to them. It's a manifestation of the abundance model.

Dr Ivan Misner, the founder of Asentiv (a consulting business focussed on referral marketing and business networking) and BNI (the largest referral organisation in the world), created the expression Givers Gain®, a philosophy that has been adopted by business owners who network worldwide.

Businesses are just the relationships between people **36**
—and between groups of people: directors and staff, marketing team and production, 'the business' and 'clients'.

Any meeting, conversation, business, job, etc can have only one purpose **45**
Because, if there appear to be two, then either one purpose is a subset of the other (so there is still only one purpose) or you are at cross-purposes, which is inefficient and confusing. Many people (in business or not) get this wrong surprisingly often.

People remember stories **58**
...they don't remember dry information. People learn when they are in their feelings, and stories are a good way of helping them get into their feelings.

The meaning of a communication is what the recipient makes of it **88**
The recipient cannot read our mind!

We already have all the resources we need **89**
This is open to interpretation. I think it is a guard against finding excuses for not starting something because we don't quite have all we think we need. In truth, we can always do something, and go at least 80% of the way with what we have. So, let's get on with it!

There is no failure, only feedback **90**
This is a belief. You may decide it's not true. I suggest believing it is true because every time we fail, we have an opportunity to learn how to do it better next time. Dodging the slew of mostly

US platitudes on this subject, here is Samuel Beckett on the subject (*Worstward Ho*):

> *Ever tried. Ever failed. No matter. Try again. Fail again. Fail better.*

Curiosity is more useful than expectation **91**
I advocate letting go of expectations, yet it is difficult to know how to fill the space they occupied (so we tend not to). I simply recommend replacing them with curiosity about what will happen now you have let go. I am not suggesting, in the first place, you do this for the rest of your life. Try for an hour first, then a day, then...

However long you think it will take, it will take longer **110**
This is just a consequence of enthusiasm, of missing out some of the things you need to do, of underestimating the time you need to do them. It's forgivable, but it does point to the value of reviewing progress against plans, not so you can beat yourself up for not achieving your goals but so that *you can do it better next time.*

There is a threshold of activity you have to reach in order to see results **111**
You would think that, however much or little you do, you would be rewarded by results in proportion to your efforts. But it seems there is a threshold over which you have to climb before you see *any* meaningful results. Unfortunately, what that threshold is depends on your business; its place in the business life cycle; the condition of the market into which you are trying to promote your wares; and your energy.

Appendix 2: Precepts of networking

The precepts of networking are 'encouragements' to do something, or think or be in a certain way.

Numbers in bold refer to topics, not pages.

Make the other person more important than you **82**
This is a fundamental precept that recurs throughout the book, in a number of guises (for example, as the definition of partnership between two business people). The crucial point is that it means, 'Act as if the other person *were* more important than you'. It does *not* mean, 'Believe that the other person is more important than you'.

I must acknowledge Chuck Spezzano and his colleagues at Psychology of Vision for introducing me to many of the principles and precepts in this book.

Deal with the world as it is, not as you would like it to be **83**
A well-known zen maxim, which is harder to put into practice than it looks, so attached are we to our beliefs that we are right about life.

Be the change you want to see in the world **84**
This well-known saying attributed to Mahatma Gandhi suggests that what we see is missing is what we are called to give. Simply, if something is missing, find a way of bringing it about.

Seek to understand the other person **85**
A cousin of the principle to deal with the world as it is: deal with people as they are, not how you think they are. Invest time and energy in discovering them.

Let go of the need to be right **86**
This is not about being right, this is about *needing* to be right (in the way that politicians need to be right), having an attachment to being right.

Feel the anxiety, and do it anyway **87**
When we are anxious about something (such as attending a networking event) it isn't really the event itself that's the problem. The problem is our anxiety that we won't be able to cope if we mess it up. This tends to result in us messing it up, thereby proving that we were right all along.

Be present **92**
We often think we really are present and only taking a moment to check our emails on our phone. But it's not enough to have got out of the car and toddled into the event: we have to devote our concentration wholly to what is going on around us, however tantalising it is to see if that prospect has replied.

Prepare well to be successful **42**
This is rather obvious, yet for many networkers, apparently, the idea of preparing for a networking event with the same care that they prepare for a meeting with a prospect is a bit of a novelty.

Be entertaining   **69**

Tell interesting stories, or any stories. They can be about clients (suitably anonymised), about you, about people you know or think you have read about (if reasonably relevant). The whole point of going to a networking event is to be remembered. Tell jokes if you have to. *If no-one remembers you, what on earth was the point in going?*

Be different   **70**

Ditto.

What does it all mean?: Glossary

In this glossary I say what I mean by key words used in this book.
Numbers in bold refer to topics, not pages.

abundance model **32**
A set of consistent beliefs that there is enough to go around and that it isn't necessary to compete with people for what we need (money, clients, friendship, approbation, love…). See *scarcity model*

advocacy **10**
Advocacy is not just referring, or even recommending; it is the ability of A to explain, often from first-hand experience, why their contact should entertain B, the person whom A is advocating. Advocacy differs from referral in that it is active and proactive, whereas referral is passive and reactive. Advocacy requires an interdependent relationship between the advocate and the one being advocated (that is, between A and B). See *interdependence*

assertiveness **130**
Assertiveness is not aggression. It is saying clearly what you want to have happen in any particular situation.

attitude **35**
Two main areas of mental processes contribute to a person's attitude towards something:

o   their feelings about that thing

o   their beliefs about it.

However, it is not an additive combination of the two, rather the complex *interaction between* these two creates a third thing, the attitude. It's feelings × beliefs, not feelings + beliefs.

authenticity **26**
Ultimately, being authentic is just being yourself, understanding that pretending to be someone else helps no-one.

behaviour cycle **31**
A model, derived from cognitive behaviour therapy, that states our behaviours are determined and driven by our feelings and emotions, and by our thoughts and beliefs. All these are, in turn, generated by our experiences (or, more accurately, by our memories of our experiences). If we want to change our behaviour, trying to change our behaviour is not usually productive: we need to change some or all of our feelings and emotions, and our thoughts and beliefs. One productive way of doing this is by having new experiences.

comfort zone **29**
Activities, beliefs and emotions which present us with no problems, but also with no challenges or stimulation.

connector **27**
Someone who knows a lot of people and enjoys connecting them together usefully. From Malcolm Gladwell's *The Tipping Point*. See *maven*

conscious, unconscious mind
You'd think from the way that people talk about our 'unconscious mind' and our 'conscious mind' that we have two minds, connected by some hitherto undiscovered pipeline. Of

course, we don't. We each have a mind. At any one time we are conscious of part of it and not conscious of the rest (probably the majority).

dead zone **40**
A stage in the relationship between two business people, following power struggle, in which each party gives up on the relationship without wanting to disengage from it.

dependence **39**
In a relationship between two people, a dependent person seeks to get all his/her needs met by the other person, rather than taking responsibility for this themselves. See *independence*, *interdependence*

elevator pitch **20**
A statement about a business cut to around thirty seconds, intended to provide a compelling reason for the listener to help the business and not succeeding.

Emotional Intelligence
The ability to identify, understand and manage one's emotions; the ability to identify, understand and influence others' emotions. Not the ability to manage others' emotions, *pace* Daniel Goleman. A values-neutral concept; emotional intelligence (EI or EQ) is neither good nor bad—it is just a set of abilities, emotions and beliefs that tend to lead to characteristic behaviours.

Further reading: Daniel Goleman, *Emotional Intelligence*.

expectation **48**
This word is used in the everyday sense of an assumption that something is going to happen, or someone is going to do something. The assumption is accompanied by a wait for the thing to happen and we can get upset if it doesn't.

giving **80**
Throughout the book, the word is used in its sense of 'unconditional giving'. 'Conditional giving' isn't giving; it's an

attempt to coerce the other person into a contract: 'I'll give you this referral, but I expect something in return'.

independence **39**
In a relationship between two people, an independent person refuses to allow the other to meet their needs, believing that they (the independent one) are the only person who can do that. Beloved of many business bosses who take the view that, 'if you want something done, you have to do it yourself', 'it's lonely at the top', and all the rest. Characterised therefore by being controlling and not trusting. Not the same as autonomy or self-sufficiency, both of which are desirable characteristics of interdependence. See *dependence, interdependence*

instinct **87**
Instinct is a predisposition to behave in certain ways in certain circumstances. Apparently, people are born with instincts, rather than acquiring them postnatally.

Instincts include 'flight or fight': when presented with immediate danger, an instinct for self-preservation kicks in; and the maternal instinct: mothers innately understand how to bring up their baby. Instinct and intuition are not the same things. See *intuition*

intention **47**
Again, this word is used in its everyday sense. I use it for short-term activities. An intention is more than a target (for example, meet three new people), it is an undertaking to oneself that we will do the best we can to achieve that target.

interdependence **39**
In a relationship between two people, an approach where each person is making the other more important than them (that is, a leadership approach), in which the person seeks to meet their own needs (hence self-sufficiency and autonomy belong here). See *leader, dependence, independence*. See also **39**.

intuition **93**
Intuition is an unconscious *rational* thinking process. As it is unconscious we are, by definition, unaware of it, and this has led people to ascribe various flaky ideas to intuition that don't stand up to scrutiny. In particular, the idea that intuition is a sense is meaningless, since it can take place without perception. See *instinct*

'*know, like and trust*' **37**
Quite simply means that A is unlikely to help B unless A knows, likes and trusts B. Often, unfortunately, forgotten.

lead **9**
A lead is someone, A, whose name (and possibly contact details) you have been given by someone else, B, who believes A could be a possible client for you or otherwise of interest. B has not taken the trouble to establish whether this is, in fact, the case. And A is probably unaware of his interest.

leader
In my book, leaders have certain characteristics that set them apart from those people who aren't leaders. Firstly, leaders are not managers, bosses or 'in charge', simply by virtue of being leaders, though it would be good if people in those three roles chose to deploy leadership characteristics.

Secondly (in my book), leaders follow the motto of the Royal Military Academy, Sandhurst, which is 'Serve to lead'. This is a classic, time-honoured and successful interpretation of leadership often called 'servant leadership'. This can be expressed in a number of ways, of which the leadership precept is the most emblematic. See *leadership precept*

leadership precept **82**
'Make the other person more important than you'. See *leader*

maven **27**
Someone who knows, and is known for knowing, a lot of stuff in specific, well-defined areas. From Malcolm Gladwell's *The tipping point*. See *connector*

network   8
A group of people and the relationships between them (think of a real net; there are the nodes and the connections between them). Each person has a relationship to at least one other. Ideally, most of them have relationships with several others in the group.

networking   5
Networking is having one-to-one meetings with individuals with whom useful business relationships could be developed. The most useful *purpose* of networking is to find out how you can help other people. However, the *point* of networking is to be remembered (if no-one remembers you, why bother?).

outcome   44
What happens as a result of achieving the purpose of a function (business, meeting, purpose and so on). See *purpose*

portfolio   53
A collection of stories, anecdotes, short presentations, jokes, comments about current affairs and other materials. Most of these should be committed to memory, but pictures and diagrams are allowed. On no account are PowerPoint presentations allowed. The value of a portfolio is that there will be occasions when you need some of that content at the tips of your fingers, *immediately*.

power struggle   40
A stage in the relationship between two business people, in which each puts satisfying their own needs before helping the other person meet theirs.

precept   6
Precepts are a particular type of principle: encouragements, suggestions, instructions to do or be something. For example, 'Be the change you want to see in the world'. See *principle*

principle **6**
A statement about how the world is. For example, 'the meaning of a message is what the recipient makes of it'. Some principles are also precepts. See *precept*

prospect **9**
A prospect is a prospective client. Someone you have some reason to know could become a client (for example, you've met them); not just anyone.

purpose **44**
Why something is done, whether it is running a business, going to a networking event or any other activity. Not the same as what happens *as a result of* achieving the purpose (these are *outcomes*), and not the same as *what is done* in order to achieve the purpose (these are *actions*).

referral **10**
When A tells B about my services, she is referring B to me (not the other way around). A should tell me that she has done this. It's preferable for her to do the introductions. For me, B is the referral. Also, the act of passing a referral.

referral relationship **10**
A worthwhile outcome of networking. It requires two business people to know enough about each other and their goods and services that each can talk credibly to third parties about the other's. Referring contains an element of recommending. The credibility issues must be addressed if the relationship is to be profitable. Unlike advocacy, which is active and proactive, referring need only be passive and reactive.

scarcity model **32**
A set of consistent beliefs that there is not enough to go around, and that 'I am not going to get enough of what I need (money, clients, friendship, approbation, love…)'. Depressingly common among business people (and not just those in small businesses). Actually, depressingly common among people full stop (it's a major driver of politicians, of course). Almost

inevitably the scarcity model is derived from early childhood experiences and beliefs and can often require will, insight and effort to transcend. See *abundance model*

selling
The activity of acquiring customers, which makes the vendor's need for the customer more important than the customer's need for particular services or products.

speed networking
A networking event apparently designed to offer the least possible benefit for the maximum anxiety.

stretch zone   **29**
A metaphorical set of activities, feelings and beliefs, outside the comfort zone, where we can be more productive and more stimulated.

subconscious mind   **88**
See *conscious mind*

Acknowledgements

There is very little in this book that is original (it's all tried and tested). The book wins by pulling together a lot of disparate ideas to create something new and useful.

I am particularly indebted to:

o Jeff Allen and Julie Wookey and their colleagues at Psychology of Vision UK for some essential ideas in the book, derived from the work of Chuck Spezzano

o Grant Leboff, for his revelatory approach to marketing

o Sarah Owen, founder of DISCsimple and co-author of *The World's Best Known Marketing Secret*, for her suggestions, interview contributions and support; Sarah read a (much longer) early version and commented very helpfully

o John Seymour, an excellent NLP trainer and author

o Darren Shirlaw of Shirlaws for his excellent training in business coaching

o Hazel Walker, best-selling author, *Business Networking and Sex*; BNI Executive Director, Indiana and British Columbia; National Training Director, BNI Australia for her help and support.

And:

o Rob Brown for prompting me to write the book in the first place

○ Martin Davies of NRG Networks for innumerable sane and civilised networking lunches, and for his suggestions and interview contributions

○ Jo Smyth, who read the whole manuscript at one stage and made many invaluable suggestions

○ many people have read the book and made valuable comments. I particularly thank my brother, Nicolas Marchant; and Warren Cass, Sue Richardson, Martin Tamlyn and Gary Weinstein for their suggestions, ideas and support

○ my publisher, Alison Jones, and Sarah Rendell and Dawn Preston; and Mark Ware

○ and Helen Braithwaite for her support.

It goes without saying that any errors and *faux pas* are of my making alone.

Further reading

Malcolm Gladwell, *The Tipping Point* (Little, Brown, 2000)
Essentially about how messages travel through communities. This is, funnily enough, exactly what the adept networker seeks to be good at bringing about.

Daniel Goleman, *Emotional Intelligence* (Bloomsbury, 1996)
Good on the subject of emotional intelligence—indeed, it was the book that was responsible for introducing the phrase into common awareness. However, it is not so hot on answering the question, 'OK, so now I am emotionally intelligent, what do I do with it?' The current book is an attempt to answer the question in the precisely defined context of business networking.

Grant Leboff, *Sales Therapy* (Capstone, 2007)
Grant Leboff, *Sticky Marketing* (Kogan Page, 2011)
These books put this current book on networking in the wider context of marketing.

Ivan Misner and Mike Macedonio, *The World's Best Known Marketing Secret* (4th edition, Beneath the Cover Press, 2011)
This book essentially covers all the procedural, thinking activities that need to be done if networking is to be a success. It neatly complements the current book.

Index of stories